Jeremiah | RESPONDING TO GOD

A.E. Heise

ISBN 978-1-950833-00-9

Published by Bees' Hive Books, Oshkosh, Wisconsin, USA.
beeshivebooks.com

Dedication

To Hoss, who has encouraged and supported me without fail.

Introduction

Dear Reader,

Thank you so much for picking up this book. There is so much depth in the book of Jeremiah and I truly hope to give you even a glimpse of it through this guide.

Although I have loved writing since I can remember, I never thought God would ask me to do it. It was always a hobby or something I worked on for school. I dreamt of seeing my name as the author of some book, but never expected it.

All that to say, I didn't write this book for me, I wrote it for a dear friend. She felt a pull towards the book of Jeremiah. God had something for her in the book, but she had trouble getting into it. In college, majoring in Religious Studies, I plodded through some fairly thick text and felt I could wade through some commentaries and make a little chapter-by-chapter guide so someone I cared about could get all that God wanted her to get out of His Word.

As I worked through the pages of Jeremiah, I sensed God wasn't using me for just one person. So many times, words struck my heart in a way that was undeniably God speaking words for me and for others. I knew then, despite my fears, I had to share this work.

Many tears have been shed over this keyboard—tears of gratitude and tears of fear. I have cried out to God, "I am too young! I can't do this." And every time He has whispered back, "For me." He has reminded me over and over again that He called me to this work for Him—for His glory, not mine. And so, I followed. Sometimes at full speed and sometimes dragging my feet, but here we are. At the finish line and yet, somehow, also at the beginning. Only God!

I have prayed for you during this process. I have asked God to move hearts with whatever words he has decided to bless me with. I pray that you would be moved. Moved to repentance. Moved to action. Moved closer to a God who has formed things in this world, both great and small, and still chooses to know us intimately. I pray that you would finish this book, finish every chapter, and respond to God.

A.E. Heise

Jeremiah 1

Jeremiah was young when he first responded to God's calling. In Jeremiah 1:6, he reminds the Lord that he does "not know how to speak, for [he is] only a youth." Many times, I have felt God tugging at my heart to lead or serve, only to tell Him, "God, I'm not old enough. Who will listen to me?" When I look back, these questioning times seem silly; God already knows and plans to use me in the midst of my doubts. Not only does He know, but He's called me to be faithful to His leading, even when I'm unsure. His answer to Jeremiah soothes that part of my heart that is so determined to turn down opportunities because of my age.

"Do not say, 'I am only a youth'; for to all to whom I send you, you shall go, and whatever I command you, you shall speak. Do not be afraid of them, for I am with you to deliver you, declares the LORD."

Jeremiah 1:7-8

God created Jeremiah for this purpose, and He informs Jeremiah of it right from the start. God has created in each of us a purpose. As He formed us, He knew everything our lives would entail and exactly how He would use us. God wasn't in the dark when He made us, therefore each of us is made very specifically for the tasks He calls us to.

Now, that's not to say He doesn't grow us or challenge us. There are plenty of things to which God has called me that I felt unfit to do at first. But He knows exactly what we're capable of and He desires to bring out the best in us; He desires to bring out traits in us He created for His glory.

Jeremiah's path was difficult. He was charged by God to warn Judah and their neighbors of the judgement God was going to bring upon them for their sins. It's no wonder Jeremiah was concerned he was too young for the job!

God never sends us out alone. God prepared Jeremiah in three ways before He sent him out.

The first was to inspire Jeremiah's words. Like Moses, Jeremiah was concerned that he could not speak God's words well. He was worried that no one would listen to him. Jeremiah attributed this insecurity to his youth, but confidence isn't guaranteed to grow with age.

Likewise, many of us worry whether we'll say the right thing, and some of us allow that fear to keep us quiet. God, instead, does something wonderful. He touches Jeremiah's lips and declares, "I have put my words in your mouth" (Jeremiah 1:9). What a glorious thought! We can ask God for the words others need to hear. We don't have to rely on our own intelligence or wit, but we can rely on the Master Communicator.

I have a special talent for putting my foot in my mouth, , and so I'm often afraid of speaking. Will I say something untrue? Will my words convey the meaning I intend? Will I say something hurtful? There are so many fears that can steal my words and keep them captive. Or, I can ask God for His touch to set my words free to be used in more ways than I could ever imagine!

After God touches Jeremiah's lips, He teaches Jeremiah about prophesy. This is the second way God prepares him. God asks Jeremiah to describe what he sees, then offers the explanation to him. God walks Jeremiah through a vision of Jerusalem's fate should the people continue to sin.

God wants to teach us. He doesn't just throw us in the deep end and see if we can swim. He wants to guide us, one step at a time, and help us through the areas where we stumble.

God has been leading me more and more into leadership. This is something I know He's given me the ability to do, but it's also something that is difficult for me. I am so thankful that He didn't throw all the roles my way at one time. Instead, He created the space for me to learn some basics, lead well in a small group of peers, and learn to rely on Him. It was after these preparations that He began putting bigger and more diverse leadership roles on my plate.

Admittedly, the subsequent roles came about more quickly. But at that point, God and I both knew that I no longer needed to crawl and was ready to walk.

The third and final thing God does for Jeremiah before sending him to anyone is the most encouraging. God builds Jeremiah into a "fortified city." To fortify means to "make strong", to "add mental...strength", and to "strengthen and secure".[1]

God strengthened Jeremiah, so he would not be defeated by those who stood against him. Jeremiah was prepared to deliver a difficult message, yet he would not face battle unprotected. God assured him that "they will fight against you, but they shall not prevail against you, for I am with you. . . .to deliver you" (Jeremiah 1:19).

God doesn't just call us to works, He prepares us for them. But He doesn't just throw us in, He waits for our response. R.K. Harrison points out, "response. . . .is the important consideration when God has spoken to man".[2] Therefore, may our response be "yes, Lord!"

Jeremiah 2

Jeremiah begins his mission. I can only imagine how difficult it must have been for him to leave his small hometown behind. His mission was to enter a city full of people and deliver a message God had sent to them. These people had spent "days without number," forgetting their God—the God of their fathers (Jeremiah 2:32). Jeremiah was called to tell the people of Judah to return to God or suffer the consequences of their sin.

God is the model of long-suffering. His bounty of patience completely boggles my mind. I'm so easily frustrated with my spouse when he doesn't seem to be paying attention to what I'm saying, either because I'm not speaking loudly enough or because he's distracted. Each time, I have to force myself to patiently repeat my words in order to keep our lines of communication open.

In contrast, though I consistently frustrate or disappoint God, He still desires to draw me closer. He doesn't focus on my failings, as I so often do, but He remembers all my moments. He sees deep value in me despite my tendency to sin.

So, God begins by calling Judah back to Him. He implores Judah to remember "the devotion of [their] youth" (Jeremiah 2:2). He reminds them of His loving care in the wilderness, when they wandered in an area where nothing could survive. He reminds them how He created springs of water from rocks and fed them daily with the miraculous manna. But He also reminds them that once they had reached the promised land, they forgot Him.

The Israelites wanted a physical king. They wanted to be like other nations, but God had chosen them to stand apart, to be His firstfruits of the nations (Jeremiah 2:3). They "defiled [God's] land and made [His] heritage an abomination" (Jeremiah 2:7). Like spoiled children, they refused to do God's will and continued to plead for what they wanted. They had forgotten all that God had done for them already.

Constantly, prophets confronted Israel and Judah with their sins, but they continued to maintain their attitude of innocence. Now, I could easily shake my finger at the Israelites and wonder, "how they could be so stubborn?!" Then, even before the words are fully formed in my thoughts, I remember my own stubbornness. It's the same stubbornness that keeps me from experiencing all the good that God wants to bestow on me. It's the same stubbornness that confounds all the lessons He wants to teach me. It's the same stubbornness that begs for what's worse for me.

Sometimes I need a gentle reminder that I too, like the Israelites, can act like a spoiled child. Distracted by sin, I find myself saying, "if some is good, more is better, and I need it now!" The Israelites were looking for more—for a seemingly better thing.

Judah wasn't simply worshiping idols—they were mixing idol worship with worship of God. Matthew Henry remarks that it was this "mixing of God's institutions with their idolatrous customs and usages, which was a great profanation [disrespect] of that which was sacred and made the ways of their idolatry worse than that of others".[3]

How many times, especially in today's age of tolerance, do we mix profanity with God's glory? I like to think that someone will get what's coming to them (karma), instead of asking God to help me forgive and show them the grace that was generously given to me.

This profanity is perhaps most noticeable in the way the world's view of sex is finding its way into our churches. Derek Kinder sees the widespread "view of sex as virtually life's chief concern and most authoritative voice—certainly one that can override the voice of God".[4] This thought seems more and more pervasive each generation. But God calls His people to be set apart. Only His way will do. No other way will suffice, nor will any shortcut.

Judah thought they could hide their pursuits of other ways from God. But God saw the murderous blood that covered them. They had slain prophets who preached the truth of God and sacrificed their children to false gods. They were dripping with the blood of innocents. And yet, before God and crimson from head to toe, they insisted they were clean. God observes, "though you wash yourself with lye and use much soap, the stain of your guilt is still before me" (Jeremiah 2:22) and "on your skirts is found the lifeblood of the guiltless poor" (Jeremiah 2:34). There is no hiding anything from Him.

God also saw their leaders, respected individuals responsible for shepherding Judah, praying to idols: "to a tree, 'You are my father,' and to a stone, 'You gave me birth.'" (Jeremiah 2:26-27). The Israelites were crediting false gods with the life, blessings, and protection God had given them. They had forgotten God's provision. They had turned to numerous other gods instead of the one true God—the only God that could meet their every need.

Jeremiah 3

It can get a bit confusing trying to keep the two kingdoms of the people of Israel straight. Let's start with some background on the Kingdoms of Israel and Judah.

Solomon was King David's son and successor, and Rehoboam was Solomon's son and successor. When Rehoboam took the throne after Solomon's death, the ten northern tribes rebelled and formed their own kingdom. The northern tribes made Jeroboam, a servant of Solomon, their king, rejecting Rehoboam as the new king. This left only the tribe of Judah, the tribe in which David and his descendants were born, and the tribe of Benjamin in the southern kingdom. The southern kingdom became known as the Kingdom of Judah. Though the kingdoms were both from the line of Abraham, Isaac, and Jacob, they were now two entities. While God's covenant still covered both, they were now politically two different nations.

In this time in Jewish culture, a man could not reunite with his wife if she left him to be with another man. Reuniting with her would cause "that land [to] be greatly polluted" (Jeremiah 3:1). Though Israel had chosen many other gods, seen as other lovers in Israel's covenant with God, God wanted Israel to return to be His again. By doing so, He shattered their cultural norms.

His desire for His children is so great that when we come to Him in repentance, He'll take us back no matter how we have defiled ourselves. He calls us to return to Him, but whether we listen is our own choice. However, like Israel and Judah, God doesn't call us once and then leave us to our demise. He calls us again and again, until we respond in repentance, and then He welcomes us with open arms. God does not just stand around twiddling His thumbs and waiting for us forever. His grace and patience are so much more than we can fathom and far more than we could ever deserve.

Despite repentance, we may still face consequences. Sin causes consequences. Though God can remove them, doing so is His choice. Sometimes, for our growth, God allows us to receive our consequences. And other times He grows us with grace.

As God is calling Israel back to Him, "a voice on the bare heights is heard, the weeping and pleading of Israel's sons" (Jeremiah 3:21). Though not all of Israel has repented, some have been filled with godly sorrow and desire to come back to Him. Not only does God hear them, but He gives them the words to repent (Jeremiah 3:22b-23).

The Holy Spirit is our helper (John 14:26). We can ask for the words to say to God, not only because He knows what's in our hearts, but because He knows what we need to hear to be moved toward change. Often when I am deep in prayer, my heart is opened to see more of God's goodness and glory. When, instead of talking at God, I allow Him to have a conversation with me, my walls are slowly broken down and I become more intimate with Him.

Often, I come before God in prayer broken, exhausted, or unsure. When I ask for God's help—or when I simply tell God that I don't have it in me, but I'll come anyway—those are the moments that I feel the Helper strengthen me and open my heart.

"Return, O faithless sons; I will heal your faithlessness."
"Behold, we come to you, for you are the LORD our God."
Jeremiah 3:22

This is a beautiful exchange. God calls out their sin, but in the same breath promises that He can heal them. He's greater than our sins. There is nothing that can defeat God, and He offers to use His strength for us. He can defeat anything we struggle with. He offers us His strength not because we deserve it, but because He loves us.

God doesn't want us to struggle through life chained to sin. Yes, we will face trials and sorrows and heartache. Yes, there will be things we struggle with for years, or even a lifetime. But God calls us to return to Him, and, when we return, He provides us with the strength to fight, moment by moment. He will never leave us where He finds us—if we let Him work on us.

When we respond to Him, He responds to us in an even mightier way. He heals us of afflictions we can't beat on our own. He helps us walk the narrow path of light and life. He doesn't abandon us to the wild things luring us off the path with false promises of ease, happiness, and lack of troubles. He whispers in our ears, "My way is better. Trust your father who loves you". And if we turn our eyes back to Him, like those few Israelites, we will be enveloped in a security that only our heavenly father can give us.

Jeremiah 4

Jeremiah warns that Judah will be overtaken by a swift army if they do not repent. This army is close, and time isn't on Judah's side. Yet Judah does not turn back to the Lord, and so suffers the consequences. God's covenant cannot be fulfilled by God only: "the steadfast love of God as expressed in the Sinai covenant must be matched by equal fidelity in the repentant people".[5] In short, the Israelites couldn't fake their way through the covenant. It had to be genuine.

Often God warns us when we wander away from Him. He may speak to us through a close friend, or the Holy Spirit might nudge us that our actions or thoughts aren't right. We get to choose to act on these warnings. God will never force us to turn back to Him, but there are consequences if we choose not to.

Judah is told to circumcise and to plow the soil of their hearts, because their hearts need to be open to receive God's warning and truly repent. Circumcision was a sign of the covenant between Israel and God. It was permanent—a symbol that could not be removed, like God's promise. Plowing soil increases its fertility. Plants might grow in unplowed soil, but plowed soil is ready for new crops. It's ready to produce. When our hearts are closed to God, whether because we're outright defiant or because we've ignored Him for so long we no longer recognize His voice, we must cultivate our hearts to hear Him again. God can certainly shout, but rarely does He raise His voice—not because He doesn't want to be heard, but because He wants us to be listening.

Children respond best when spoken to calmly and firmly. God is the example of a perfect father. He doesn't scream at us or beat us into submission. He speaks firmly and gently to us. To hear Him, we must listen attentively.

If we don't train ourselves to listen to God, it is much more difficult to hear Him. Especially in this noisy world, it's easy for God's voice to be drowned out and pushed down. When we listen for Him His voice rises to the top. And the more we respond to His voice, the easier it is to recognize it.

Jeremiah goes on to question God about other prophets. "Surely you [God] have utterly deceived this people and Jerusalem, saying 'It shall be well with you,' whereas the sword has reached [Judah's] very life" (Jeremiah 4:10). False prophets gave Judah this promise—but because of their idolatry Judah could not recognize them as false. And when the time came for the priests and prophets to encourage the people, which was part of their job during times of war, they spread terror instead.

Jeremiah was a true prophet, and spoke true messages from God. But those messages spoke of consequences and destruction. The people chose the teachings of false prophets—pleasant teachings that required no action. Judah assumed they could live this way and God would still protect them.

We're exceptional at living a la carte. We love to pick and choose the rules by which we live, especially when it comes to religion. Social media is littered with feel-good statements about peace and love from famous religious leaders and speakers. However, there aren't many difficult messages about obedience, responsibility, or developing character.

God doesn't want us to follow His commandments because we like them better than the alternatives. He wants us to follow His commandments because we love Him so much that we're willing to give up our comforts to be made more like Him. He wants our security and our joy to come from Him, so sometimes He tells us hard truths to call us back when we are pulled away. He wants to shower us in goodness—not goodness in a worldly sense, but godly goodness in which our lives may glorify Him.

God wants us to hear His difficult messages so we can also hear His most beautiful message, "Well done, my good and faithful servant" (Matthew 25:21).

Jeremiah 5

The sound of God's heart breaking is almost audible after endless chapters of Judah's sin. His children refused to turn away from or even attempt to see their sin. Idolatry is a cozy sin, and they were content in it.

Idolatry puts us in control, since our idols have no real power. They have no ability to change seasons or direct our path as God does. This makes them feel safe. We get wrapped up in them and entrust our hearts to them. Idols only have what power we give them; they can't take anything we don't truly want to give up.

Idolatry sneaks up on us. Social media can be both a channel for idols and an idol itself. It's easy to get wrapped up in perceptions on the Internet especially. Perhaps not even consciously, we come to believe someone has it all figured out. Rather than following God, we model our lives after their curated image. How often do we find ourselves fishing for comforting words and solutions to our problems online? And we certainly don't want to disappoint or mess up in front of our digital friends. It's a slippery slope.

Idolatry can creep into our relationships, too. It's important to have people to confide in when we're struggling and to help pick us up when we've fallen. But, when sharing our heart in that relationship is more important to us than trusting in God and relying on Him, or when that person becomes the center of our life, we cross a line.

Because of their covenant relationship with God, Judah's idolatry looked a lot like adultery. They no longer wanted God to be their security, provision, or most intimate connection. They desired to be like other nations. They sought earthly gain instead of the eternal treasures of God.

In college I veered onto Judah's path. Even though I was active in my church and campus ministry, I was stuck in a perpetual loop of sin and sorrow. Daily, I would cry out to God, "Why are you doing this to me? Why won't you change things?" I felt trapped, unable to get out of the whirlpool I was creating.

I craved love and acceptance. I craved beauty and to be desired. I craved security and arms to hold me. I searched for it everywhere. I yelled at God, "You haven't helped! You're leaving me lonely!" I felt like I would be searching forever, but over time He helped open my eyes to the sin I couldn't see right in front of me. I idolized an earthly relationship and overrule my relationship with God. But God, His ever-patient self, kept calling me, gently, but firmly. He refused to give me over to my sin. He had other plans for my life—not obstinacy, but repentance.

It took years to truly get out of my whirlpool and He allowed consequences, but He wouldn't let sin completely consume me. Looking back, I see His hand protecting me in so many ways despite my idolatry.

He wouldn't let Judah be consumed by their sin either. He'd allow their circumstances to worsen if they refused to repent, but He wouldn't let everyone die. The nation would survive, and He'd continue to call them back to Him. He refused to "make a full end" of them (Jeremiah 5:18).

God doesn't just let His children walk out on Him. He calls us back repeatedly. He desires our repentance and our homecoming. He reaches out to us, but He doesn't stand in our way or force us to stay.

God also wants our respect. He will not be a doormat. We don't get to walk all over His commands and then cry, "uncle!" to make the consequences disappear. God wants us to walk His path of righteousness. This requires discipline, self-control, and respect for Him. Respecting Him means placing nothing above Him, nor replacing Him. Anything supplanting our respect of Him is an idol and He will call us out on it, as He did Judah. But He is also ready to accept our heartfelt repentance and restore us.

Jeremiah 6

While God's repeated and unanswered call to Judah is heartbreaking, Judah's stubbornness is monotonous and tiresome. I don't know how God had so much patience with Judah. Just reading about their refusal to turn back to Him is exhausting. But God is so good and does not hand us over to our sin. He continues to call after us with unmatchable forbearance.

But even as He calls us, He sometimes hands us over to our consequences. Judah refused to repent. In fact, they didn't believe that they were doing anything wrong in the first place. They believed their false prophets who shouted "peace, peace". They had fallen so far "they were not at all ashamed; they did not know how to blush" (Jeremiah 6:15), even in the face of God's rebukes.

Living in this fallen world, it's easy to avoid the holy guilt of sin. We want to be true to ourselves, to follow our heart, and to find happiness—because that's the best the world has to offer: the pursuit of happiness. But as Christians we're called above all that. We're called to be true to God, to follow His commands, and to give Him glory above all else. Then we will find what God wants us to experience—joy.

The Holy Spirit places a godly sorrow in our hearts towards sin, which when we repent turns to joy. But we can quench this feeling. When we ignore and deny conviction so much we don't feel it, we risk losing our ability to spiritually blush. We also miss out on the joy of refreshing our relationship with God (Acts 3:20).

It took me a long time to be willing to blush before God. He'd remind me of a current or past unrepented sin and instead of embracing the blush, I would pretend the sin didn't exist. I would push it back into the recesses of my mind. I hated that feeling of conviction. It made me feel worthless and full of worldly shame. Then a friend told me about 2

Corinthians 7:10, which says, "for godly grief produces a repentance that leads to salvation without regret, whereas worldly grief produces death."

Giving my life to Jesus and acknowledging Him as my savior is my only source of salvation. But maintaining a God-centered life requires a constant searching of my heart for sin and repenting from it. Without this rhythm of confession and repentance, my spiritual fruit will dry up and die. The term fruit is used throughout scripture to represent the good that develops in or from the heart of a Christian. When we live in sin we cannot produce fruit. We need God's careful and gentle tending to our lives to bear fruit, and that is only possible through spiritual intimacy with Him (John 15:5).

It's easy to hear this call to intimacy, and to instead move towards spiritual duties motivated by obligation. But God doesn't want our rituals, He wants our intimacy. He wants us to walk with Him personally and to learn from Him. There are some rituals we do to help us remember what God has done for us, or to demonstrate our understanding of His love for us. But when "[r]itual performances are divorced from a proper moral attitude [they] are worthless in God's sight".[6] When we take communion just to be part of the ritual without also searching our hearts for the unconfessed or hidden sin that may lie there, we're not rightly motivated.

When we don't acknowledge our sins, and we run from blushing before God, we slowly kill the fruit of our lives. The fruit will neither die nor grow in abundance overnight. Both take time. Therefore, the more often we allow ourselves to blush before God, and the more often we repent, the more often we will bear fruit and experience incredible intimacy with God.

Judah repeatedly refused to blush, and by doing so lost the war coming to them before it even started. God spends most of this chapter detailing what they will lose at the hands of the Chaldeans. Though this isn't their last chance to repent, Jeremiah warns them of the coming consequence so when it comes they will know the warning was from God.

Jeremiah 7

Though Judah is condemned to destruction, it can't be said they are innocent victims. God clearly informs His people as to why they were facing such consequences. With each new chapter, more of Israel's sin is revealed, as is God's continual call for repentance.

Their love of idols wasn't the worst of their idolatry; the worst was believing they could love idols and yet still enjoy God's grace simply by going to the temple. Because God dwelled at the temple, they believed they had His favor. It's similar to when we try to make up for our sin by going to church, as though He'll forgive us just for being in His house.

God does want to forgive us, but God is not simple-minded and is never fooled by insincere apologies. He sees through our masks. Those who truly repent turn away from the sin. Though they may fall short again, they take tangible steps to eradicate the sin from their life.

When we truly repent, we become more aware of the situations we allow ourselves to be a part of, the words we let out of our mouth, and the thoughts we permit to race around in our mind. As we bring those things under control, with God's help, we're able to follow His path more faithfully. Neither stabilizing blood sugars nor purging a particular sin from our lives happens overnight. But if next year we're working on the same sin from the same place we have to consider whether we're really fighting that sin or just trying to look like we are.

Judah sought to use the temple for sanctuary from the God whose presence dwelled inside it. They were trying to escape the consequences of their sins by acting like good religious folks. Their "temple worship was little better than a charm for averting evil".[7] It's the same as someone believing religious artifacts can offer some sort of protection.

God is personal. He doesn't dwell in places to be our good luck charm against evil. He dwells in us so that we may experience His glory and reflect it here.

Judah still gave their offerings regularly, offerings that should have been pleasing to God. Instead He tells them to keep them. He tells them to "add [their] burnt offerings to [their] sacrifices and eat the flesh" (Jeremiah 7:21). He finds no pleasure in placative rote offerings. He reminds them that He gave their forefathers one command when He brought them out of Egypt, "Obey my voice" (Jeremiah 7:23). All other commands serve this one command, including instructions for sacrifices. Without obedience they could not glorify God, so their offerings would be more useful as dinner.

When we serve out of obligation or for show we miss out on the joy of serving. Only obedient servitude pleases and glorifies God. If our relationship with God is distant or obscured by sin, what we do in His name doesn't honor Him. But those same acts of service done from an honest and intimate relationship with God bring Him the most glory.

God desires our obedience more than any religious act we could perform. As much as He loves our worship, worship from a body consumed by sin offends Him. God is deeply grieved when we strive for looks but are falling apart on the inside because we refuse to come to Him and repent. He bids us: return to Him and be mended. We must choose to respond.

Jeremiah 8

Therefore I will give their wives to others
and their fields to conquerors,
because from the least to the greatest
everyone is greedy for unjust gain;
from prophet to priest,
everyone deals falsely.
They have healed the wound of my people lightly,
saying, 'Peace, peace,'
when there is no peace.

Jeremiah 8:10-11

The Israelites had been blessed not only with the Word, but also with prophets and priests who could lead them under God's direction. Unfortunately, those prophets and priests became corrupt. The prophets spoke false words of peace and fortune, the priests fell in love with money, and all the while the people fell into idolatry.

In reading the book of Jeremiah, we see humanity's long history of fixing up God's words. What God says can be hard to hear. There are moments of intense judgment that would certainly be easier to hear if rephrased as light discipline. But such alterations would be a disservice to ourselves and a slap in the face to God. It's as if to say our knowledge is higher than His.

There are many people still today teaching peace and happiness in God's name, and it is our responsibility to discern who is trying to please us and who is trying to teach us. It can be hard work, but it's important that we test everything we hear against God's perfect Word.

If someone says something that strikes me as wrong, I try to research it, especially if they reference the Bible or God. Ideally, I should double check every single idea proposed to me against the Bible. We have the Word in our hand for a reason; it is a guide and truth that does not change.

We need to take the ideas of every leader and speaker with a grain of salt. We need to know they are listening to the Holy Spirit, doing their research, and that they won't sugar coat difficult truths. And even then, we still need to assess the validity of every thought they communicate. Plenty of teachers, even well-intentioned ones, will, like a false prophet, tell us what we want to hear. We must be vigilant and know the Scripture for ourselves so as not to take the same path as Judah.

Theologian Derek Kidner writes, "Not content with wandering like sheep we go off at the gallop (6b); and theologically we may use our cleverness to trim the word of God (8) or to reject it outright (9)…[but] there is nothing to choose between perverting Scripture and discarding it. In the act of 'mending the oracles of God' we deny their divine status".[8] We can choose to deny or change scripture, but it comes at a very heavy cost (Revelation 22:18).

Jeremiah 9

Jeremiah continues pleading for Judah to repent, "Oh that my head were waters and my eyes a fountain of tears, that I might weep day and night for the slain of the daughter of my people!" (Jeremiah 9:1) He feels deeply for his people. He wants desperately to see them turn away from their destruction.

I spent years trying to desensitize my heart because it was always being broken by this world. But God wants us to feel one another's pain. He wants us to carry one another's burdens. He wants us to empathize with the struggles of others, because in doing so, we experience His heart.

Only when my heart is broken do I pour myself into prayer and cling to God, asking for His comfort for those who are suffering. When I find a situation only mildly sad or upsetting, I tend to quickly move on. But when my heart is breaking, I stop whatever I'm doing to pray. I plead with God on behalf of those for whom my heart breaks.

As I've aged, I've realized it's okay to have a sensitive heart. As I've grown with God, I've also learned that a burdened heart is wonderful. It's beautiful to cry for strangers over the tragedies in the news. There's something about experiencing sorrow for and with others that brings us into connection with them and with God's heart.

Jeremiah understood and felt the connection that comes from feeling burdened for others. Jeremiah was likely hoping that his fellow countrymen would see his burden for them and be moved by what his words.[9] He wanted them to know he wasn't acting superior; he was trying to share God's message so they could be saved. He longed for Judah to weep over their sins.

Unfortunately, Judah leans on yet another religious act thinking it will save them—circumcision. They believe that this sign of the covenant (which all Israelite men have) will bring assurance of salvation. But God calls them out, "the house of Israel are uncircumcised in heart" (Jeremiah

9:26). God was looking at their heart, not their bodies or actions, to see whether they truly loved Him.

The act of circumcision was meant to be an outward sign of the Israelites' covenant with God, displaying their belonging to Him. Instead, it was being used as justification.[10] When we perform spiritual acts without our hearts behind it, the act becomes meaningless. Judah became like surrounding nations who were "circumcised meaninglessly in a rite which was thus no better than a mutilation (as Paul would put it in Phil. 3:2)".[11]

Ouch. How easy it is for my actions to not match the condition of my heart. I want everything I do to be meaningful and to reflect God's glory. This is easiest to achieve by following God's instruction:

> *Thus says the Lord, "Let not the wise man boast in his wisdom, let not the mighty man boast in his might, let not the rich man boast in his riches, but let him who boasts boast in this, that he understands and knows me, that I am the Lord who practices steadfast love, justice, and righteousness in the earth. For in these things I delight, declares the Lord."*
>
> *Jeremiah 9:23-24*

Judah attempted to boast in their circumcision, and in living near the temple of the Lord. But neither could bring salvation. Judah needed to repent to come back under God's protection. This verse reminds me that it's not what I do or know that qualifies me for salvation. Only by my repentance and surrender does God save me.

Jeremiah 10

It is believed that this prophesy was given after the Chaldeans took at least some of Judah into captivity. Jeremiah is lamenting the taking of his brothers and sisters. However, those remaining in Judah still refuse to repent and are therefore subject to the same fate. Jeremiah reminds them their idolatry got them into this mess, and if they refuse to give up their idols, they will suffer the consequences.

Jeremiah also tears down the idols Judah has been worshiping. He places the reality of their mute idols up against their living covenant with God. He reminds the people that these false gods are merely "the work of the craftsman and of the hands of the goldsmith" (Jeremiah 10:9). Judah gave works of their hands—idols—the position of creator in their hearts.

Our culture also reveres idols. Some are obvious, like the Buddha statue on my neighbor's porch. Others are more subtle. Though we may not have manmade images in our homes, it's still deceptively easy to fall into worshiping creation and not the creator. The easiest trap to fall into, for Judah and for us, is the worship of art. Devoted fans are desperate to know what their favorite artist says, does, likes and dislikes. But should that artist be exposed as less than perfect, those fans feel as though it happened to them personally. That's when enjoying becomes idolizing.

When I look at nature I am in awe. Nature doesn't sustain itself; it completely depends on God. A flower is stunning because it was sculpted by God, is taken care of by God, and is used by God to remind us of Him. Nature calls out His name, whether or not we want to hear it. Nature points to God and is compelled to worship Him even when we fail to do so.

That is why it is such an abomination for us to worship created things. It goes against their very nature to be worshiped. God gave us beautiful things in this life, but we must never forget where they came from.

We should marvel at the works of God's hands. But when we put the sun, moon, stars or any other object or person in God's place, enjoying has become idolizing. We are meant to enjoy creation, but the most beautiful aspect of created things is their creator—God.

Jeremiah 11

The Lord has called Judah continuously, but they stubbornly refuse to listen. They continue to live in their sin and fight for their idols. And now we hear the dreaded words, "Therefore do not pray for this people, or lift up a cry or prayer on their behalf, for I will not listen when they call to me in the time of their trouble" (Jeremiah 11:14).

Those words fill me with such sorrow. There are too many people in my life, friends and family, who are in love with their sin. Could a time come when God would ask me to stop praying for someone I love? After all, I was stuck there, too.

I pray hardest for those people because when I was there, I needed prayer. But I also know if they refuse to listen to God—if they refuse to respond to His call—there is nothing I can do for them. They need to make their own choice to repent and come to God.

Judah is so against Jeremiah's message that they set a trap for him in his hometown. The men of Anathoth, whom Jeremiah grew up with, are determined to kill him because of their frustration with him. They plan to "destroy the tree with its fruit" and "cut him off from the land of the living, that his name be remembered no more" (Jeremiah 11:19).

But God has other plans. He alerts Jeremiah to their plot. In turn, Jeremiah asks God for justice against those who scheme to destroy him. He desires to continue God's work, because he knows it's not finished yet. God brings the men of Anathoth to justice for their plot, protects His prophet, and continues to use him to bring the truth to Judah.

It's our fallen nature to shrink away from the truth. The truth isn't always easy. It's not fluffy and comfy; sometimes it even hurts. The truth can cause us to move from where we are to where God wants us to be. When we fill ourselves with truth, God's glory can shine through us.

Our world loves fluffy ideas—especially useless ones. And it's not new; the prophets in Judah were experts. They spoke frivolously and pleasantly of peace and happiness, in direct opposition to God's warnings. They were wrong but wouldn't admit it. They simply weren't willing to put in the work the truth required.

It can be so easy for us to try to avoid ruffling feathers, saying only what others want to hear. Or worse, we can bend the truth, even slightly, so that it'll be softer on others' ears. But when we try to twist and shape truth into something easier for others to receive, it is no longer truth.

We are called to broadcast truth. If we do, some people will be angry at us. If we do, we may lose some friends or even family. But truth is worth so much more. It's worthy of eternity. And if we spread truth the way God calls us to, not only will many be given an opportunity to experience a relationship with God, but those who previously refused the truth may have a second or third chance to accept it. Jeremiah did exactly as God told him, and it certainly wasn't easy. But the intimacy he gained with God was so worth it. Ours will be too.

Jeremiah 12

Take a deep breath and buckle up. This chapter hits on some difficult truths we must touch on to truly understand the God we serve. Don't be afraid of doubts that arise; share them and work them out with God. He knows your heart, He knows your fears, and He wants to help you understand these difficult truths. Let Him.

These first twelve chapters have been stuffed with the sins of Judah. The long list angers God and so He sends Jeremiah calling for repentance. God describes Judah's trespasses in detail, as well as the pain He feels watching His children fall away.

If there's one thing that can be hard to admit, it's that God isn't only merciful, He's also always just. He doesn't let the criminal off just because that criminal is His child. He disciplines His children for their growth and His glory.

> *"She has lifted up her voice against me; therefore I hate her."*
> *Jeremiah 12:8*

This verse cuts me to the core. "She" refers to all of Israel and her blatant disregard for God. The most convicting part is the phrase, "therefore I hate her." I know God is abundantly loving, and cares for me more than I could ever imagine or understand. However, this verse reminds me that what I say and do matters.

I wonder just how much I hurt God when I sin. I wonder how much pain I cause Him with thoughtless words. I wonder how much pain I cause Him when I give up instead of relying on Him. I wonder how much it hurts Him when I choose what I want instead of what He asks.

I also wonder if God has ever said this about me. I've sinned. I know I've hurt God. Has God ever said He hated me?

My reassurance is this: God gave His only Son for me. He sent Jesus to die a horrendous death on the cross so that I could join His family. Jesus stood in my place, while I was still a sinner, so He could take on God's wrath for me. When I inevitably fall short, He asks for my repentance because He desires reconciliation, not because I have to be saved again.

He's always pulled me close and whispered how much He loves me, and then shouted it, and then whispered it once more, burying it deep in my heart. He's affirmed His love in such a way that the next time sin comes knocking, I might remember who my father is and not open the door. I might fail against temptation, but I must always repent. No one can or will love me like God.

God is fully just, and by design He is the supreme judge of this world. But the good news is He makes life with Him in eternity attainable and available for everyone. The very end of this chapter holds that wonderful promise for those nations around Judah.

"And after I have plucked them up, I will again have compassion on them, and I will bring them again each to his heritage and each to his land. And it shall come to pass, if they will diligently learn the ways of my people, to swear by my name, 'As the Lord lives,' even as they taught my people to swear by Baal, then they shall be built up in the midst of my people."

Jeremiah 12:15-16

God extends His hand not just to Judah, but even to the surrounding countries who influenced His people to turn away. His mercy is beautiful. But His justice must never be forgotten.

Jeremiah 13

God's message to Judah doesn't just fall on deaf ears, but ears that deafen further as He speaks. They have already endured one bout of captivity. Despite His continued warnings, Judah believes they're out of danger.

Jeremiah has been abundantly faithful to God so far. At the beginning of this chapter he takes a two-week journey[12] at God's word—twice! His life has been threatened, his hometown despises him, he's followed God's every command and it has amounted to only suffering. But he continues, for the love of and devotion to God, and the love for his brothers and sisters of Judah.

> *But if you will not listen, my soul will weep in secret for your pride; my eyes will weep bitterly and run down with tears, because the Lord's flock has been taken captive.*
>
> *Jeremiah 13:17*

This isn't the first time we've heard Jeremiah weeping for those who refuse to listen. His tears are far from the last spilled by people of God broken hearted over the lost.

It's okay to cry for those who are lost. Having spent too much of my life teaching myself not to cry, I've missed out on crying for those I care about. Our private misery—not crying for show, but out of true sorrow—can be a prayer in its own right.

Crying is therapeutic. It's a wonderful way to connect with God. In our sadness we desire comfort, and where better to find it than from our heavenly father. We are made in God's image, including our emotions. God wants us to come to Him, especially with our pain.

Jeremiah was crying for Judah, but he was also crying for God. God's heart was breaking as Judah continued to ignore Him. I don't know how God experiences grief, but I can imagine He feels it far more deeply than we do.

We have opportunities daily, even hourly, to grieve God or to honor Him. The choice to honor Him isn't always easy. It's a choice—a choice to avoid the line of sin instead of seeing how close we can get. The devil will always be trying to distract us, even more so it seems when we are aligned with God. In these moments we need to rely on the Holy Spirit.

God chose a loincloth as the first sign to Judah in this chapter. As it is an undergarment, a loincloth clings closely to the body. Judah was to be that loincloth to God. "God had wanted [Judah] to cling to Him in loyalty and faith, but instead she had shaped her destiny of ruin through intimacy with pagan deities".[13]

We get to choose to what we cling. If we choose wrong we become that soiled loincloth, fit only to be thrown out.

Jeremiah 14

Due to drought, farmers are "cover[ing] their heads" (Jeremiah 14:3) in shame because they cannot plow the land and grow crops. These are dire times for Judah. Everyone and everything is suffering. This is yet another consequence of Judah's sins.

> *The Lord said to [Jeremiah]: "Do not pray for the welfare of this people. Though they fast, I will not hear their cry, and though they offer burnt offering and grain offering, I will not accept them. But I will consume them by the sword, by famine, and by pestilence."*
>
> *Jeremiah 14:11*

The nation of Judah has forgotten their God and given Him up for idols. As a nation, they have decided to follow the pagan ways of their neighbors instead of staying in covenant with God. God does not force us to choose Him.

Jeremiah has been so faithful to God. We see glimpses of Jeremiah begging God to change His mind, yet Jeremiah remains faithful while watching his nation suffer—first from invasion and now from famine. He knows this is only the start because he knows if Judah continues to refuse God, they will suffer more consequences. He knows God is just, is merciful, and has a complete plan.

Talking to God, Jeremiah brings up the prophets falsely assuring Judah they'll "not see the sword, nor shall [they] have famine" (Jeremiah 14:13). God assures Jeremiah,

> *"Therefore thus says the Lord concerning the prophets who prophesy in my name although I did not send them, and who say, 'Sword and famine shall not come upon this land': By*

sword and famine those prophets shall be consumed. And the people to whom they prophesy shall be cast out in the streets of Jerusalem...."

Jeremiah 14:15-16

This stuck out to me as a reminder that God does not take lightly those who offer false security in His name. Nor does He ignore those who readily accept what they hear as from God without first checking its validity. It's far too easy to say, "God will take care of you" to comfort someone when we may or may not know that to be true.

Yes, God is our greatest comforter, protector, and our most trustworthy provider. But He is also just. Unless I'm certain I've been given the words to speak, it's not fair of me to speak pleasantries in God's name. It puts the wrong idea in our heads—the idea that God is our fairy godmother who will always take care of us in the specific way that we ask, just because we ask, whether or not we are obeying Him.

Jeremiah petitioned God to remember his people. God answered "no" repeatedly—not because God didn't love Judah, but because Judah was taking advantage of their covenant. They were relying on their special position as God's people to avoid suffering, instead of obeying the Law.

God is so willing to and so wants to forgive Judah. Judah continues to offer burnt and grain offerings, to fast and to pray, but there is no heart behind it. They are just going through the motions. They are trying to hold onto God's promises while living in their sins.

Judah was trying to do as little work as possible to stay in God's covenant. How often do we try to use ritual or deeds to please God instead of surrendering ourselves to Him for His glory?

Jeremiah 15

Jeremiah's complaints linger. He complains of those who hate him for the truth he speaks. He's been faithful to God and persecuted for it, but his role as a prophet is starting to wear on him.

Cursing his own birth, he laments, "woe is me, my mother, that you bore me, a man of strife and contention to the whole land! I have not lent, nor borrowed, yet all of them curse me." (Jeremiah 15:10)

Do I hear a child? Is someone having a meltdown in the candy aisle? Or is it me, complaining about my circumstances? Ouch.

None of us could blame Jeremiah for his growing bitterness. We often take on service commitments with more selfish motives than we recognize, but this quickly turns to resentment when our unvoiced expectations go unmet.

But this is what God has prepared Jeremiah for. God told Jeremiah in the very first chapter that He'd make him like a fortress, and now He reminds him.

> *"And I will make you to this people*
> *a fortified wall of bronze;*
> *they will fight against you,*
> *but they shall not prevail over you,*
> *for I am with you*
> *to save you and deliver you,*
> *declares the Lord."*

Jeremiah 15:20

When we place our faith in Christ we take on a similar calling—a calling to share God with a world who doesn't want to listen to Him. But He never sends us alone. We have the God of the universe indwelling us through the Holy Spirit.

We're not meant to be friends with this world, but we're meant to glorify God in it. Our calling puts us up against the things the world deems permissible that God does not. Living out this calling will not be easy, but when we rely on God for strength we can persevere.

It's okay to be at the beginning of the race. Jeremiah had to struggle with the pain of rejection, and we all do at some point in our lives. In Jeremiah's struggle, God promises that if he continues to speak "what is precious, and not what is worthless, [he] shall be as [God's] mouth" (Jeremiah 15:19).

God had already provided Jeremiah with the words, and then He also refreshed Jeremiah. In Jeremiah's despair, God took the time to remind him of the promises he was sent with.

Jeremiah 16

God instructs Jeremiah to abstain from having a family as well as from entering the houses of mourning or feasting. These refer to the two large gatherings in Jewish culture, funerals and weddings. It's common in Jewish culture for family and friends to sit with those who are mourning in their homes. Similarly, the Jewish wedding tradition was to fill the house to the brim with guests and have a lengthy feast in celebration of the marriage. Both events were very important socially.

The business of mourning is important even today. People who don't attend a funeral without a good reason are considered thoughtless. The number of people who pay their respects reflects the deceased person's level of importance. We tend to associate large funeral attendance with being a popular person.

The same goes for a wedding. Large, expensive weddings demand attention. They're a show of wealth. Big weddings were similar in Jeremiah's day. Hosting these events wasn't the only way to gain some notoriety. Attending them was also an honor. It stands out that Jeremiah was commanded by God to not celebrate his friends and family getting married or to celebrate their life through traditional mourning.

I've learned God sometimes asks us to do strange things. Samuel thought it odd that God asked him to anoint David king out of all his strapping brothers. David was scrawny and unimpressive to Samuel's human eyes. But he obeyed, and David was one of the few godly kings Israel had. He might ask us to speak to someone we've never met and may never see again. Or He may ask us to not see a specific movie, even if it doesn't seem sacrilegious.

God didn't say everyone was to stay single and not mourn with their family. Only Jeremiah received this instruction, as a symbol of Judah's loneliness as long as they refused to repent.[14] Sometimes we end up in places were God will ask us to do or not do certain things because of location, or the people in that place.

God doesn't always ask for our obedience for our own sakes. We're lights to this world, and sometimes we're asked to be brighter lights to specific people.

Jeremiah 17

Jeremiah has faithfully delivered God's message to Judah regarding their sin. Yet, in the previous chapter Judah wonders what they have done to deserve this. Now, through Jeremiah, God tells them yet another time what their sins are.

"The sin of Judah is written with a pen of iron; with a point of diamond it is engraved on the tablet of their heart, and on the horns of their altars, while their children remember their altars and their Asherim, beside every green tree and on the high hills, on the mountains in the open country. Your wealth and all your treasures I will give for spoil as the price of your high places for sin throughout all your territory."

Jeremiah 17:1-3

What a permanent catalog of sin. There is no erasing what a diamond tip has engraved. Many layers must be sanded down to remove all traces of it. Indeed, "the sin of sinners is never forgotten until it is forgiven".[15]

This description provides some fresh insight about sin. Nothing can remove sin until it is forgiven, and sin is painful to God. He hates it with all of His being. Once covered by Christ's blood, God sees Him in my place for eternity. But sin that I let into my life will still cause a rift between us. They cause me to pull away, intentionally or unintentionally. Sins from which I'm too stubborn to ask forgiveness and turn away are etched on the tablet of my heart. Once etched, they can't be erased until I am willing to repent and accept that forgiveness.

Judah refuses. They continue to pain God with their sin. And yet while hurting, God doesn't want to see them destroyed; He wants the people of Judah to ask for forgiveness and come back to Him. Jeremiah felt the same way. In public he obediently prophesies their destruction, but in private, he begs God to spare them and give them more time.

We so desire to see hearts and lives changed. We can pray for our loved ones and for the world to change, but if we try to make that change happen by ourselves, we will burn out. Only God can change hearts. Jeremiah was exhausted by Judah's stubbornness, but he continued to trust that God's plan was best.

Being a Christian means being different. We will face heartache and difficult situations with people we love and care about. But God will never leave us to face this world alone. He wants to give us strength and wisdom to make it through those painful and difficult times. When we stay committed to truth through every difficult thing, as Jeremiah did, our relationship with God grows and deepens.

Jeremiah 18

God uses word pictures and analogies to help us understand Him and His ways. The infinity of God is tough to fully understand (my brain hurts just considering it), and word pictures and analogies help us think about Him in a more tangible way.

God wants us to know Him, and that's why He gave us the Bible. It's a tool to get to know Him better—even the difficult aspects. This chapter includes a great analogical example.

> *"Arise, and go down to the potter's house, and there I will let you hear my words."*
>
> *Jeremiah 18:2*

Jeremiah was probably aware of the process of pottery making. It is suggested that God sent Jeremiah to make "the idea of it fresh in his mind" when God used it as an analogy.[16]

Nature is a wonderful way to bring God's glory fresh to our minds. Watching small birds find food or leaves swaying in the breeze can remind us of how capable God is and how much He cares about His creation. He promises to not forsake a little bird. How much more does He promise to not forsake His child?

There's something hands-on about the reminder that God is intimately involved with our lives and is shaping them continuously. I have free will, but God shapes me when I give my decisions to Him and obey His Spirit.

So I went down to the potter's house, and there he was working at his wheel. And the vessel he was making of clay was spoiled in the potter's hand, and he reworked it into another vessel, as it seemed good to the potter to do.

Jeremiah 18:3-4

Because clay is malleable, a potter can shape it as he wills. And he does so, not with malice, but lovingly. "This craftsman is no plodding amateur: his touch has the boldness and resource of the true artist, and we can extrapolate from the immediate setting of the parable, to reflect God's maturely remaking [of people]...."[17]

One side of this parable is the uplifting thought of God's power to change plans and shift intentions. However, as God reveals to Jeremiah, He can do this to bless His people, or to discipline them. God has the power to destroy any nation. He is the master of the clay. If the clay is marred or damaged, He can rework it or even dispose of it as He sees fit.

This is where the wonder of our God is on display. When a master works with clay, their movements are precise and firm. But they're also delicate—even when they're reshaping the clay. It's a pliable substance, so someone who knows what they're doing can rework it without damage.

As the universal executor of justice, God must repay sin with wrath. But He gives His children more time than would even the most patient human father before He allows our consequences to fall upon us. No matter how big or small the transgression, He wants us to come to Him first.

Jeremiah 19

"There is no fleeing from God's justice but by fleeing to [God's] mercy".[18]

Judah has been given countless chances to repent, to turn from their ways and come back to God. In doing so they could avert the coming destruction. Alas, from denial to bargaining, it's clear they'd try anything to avoid admitting their wrongs.

Jeremiah is sent to the Topheth, or the Valley of Hinnom, a place full of idolatrous sacrifices and later, the remains of criminals. He went with several elders to give a visual representation of God's planned destruction[19], hoping their accompaniment would deeply move those who were present in Topheth and as well as those who later heard of this trip.

In the previous chapter, God sent Jeremiah to the potter in order to give him a visual representation of God's power. In this chapter, Jeremiah uses one of the potter's creations to give Judah a visual representation of God's justice.

"Thus says the Lord of hosts: So will I break this people and this city, as one breaks a potter's vessel, so that it can never be mended...."

Jeremiah 19:11

Jeremiah smashes the potter's creation. God is now demonstrating to Judah what He showed Jeremiah—He, God over all, has the power to completely demolish His creation. They've been given chances to repent, but once the consequences begin, they'll become like the hardened clay vessels, "beyond reconstruction and only fit for breaking".[20]

God uses creation to move our hearts. Art can be a very powerful visual representation of God's character and capabilities. Paintings, songs, plays, novels, and dance can all take the place of the potter's creation as a novel illustration of some facet of God. God gives us creative talents to steward for His glory. This gift is meant to be used to point ourselves and others back to the ultimate Creator.

The Valley of Hinnom, where Jeremiah was sent, was significant as well. At this place Judah sacrificed and offered as burnt offerings their children to Baal and Molech. It was one of the most heinous parts of their idolatry. After the altars were torn down, it was used to cremate criminals. Part of the reason God brought them to this place was to connect their unacceptable sacrifice and unconsecrated death with their own promised destruction. [21]

God uses our memories to spur us to repentance—sometimes gently, sometimes more bluntly. It depends on our willingness to confront the memory, admit the sin, and ask for forgiveness.

I can't blame Judah for trying to find another way out. They surely wanted to forget what they did, and so either repressed the memories or normalized the actions. But even so, the horrible things they did would surely have clawed at them from the corners of their consciousness.

It's not easy to repent. Often, it's absolutely heart wrenching. But the resulting grace and mercy God pours out on those who repent instead of fight is incredibly freeing.

Jeremiah 20

Pashhur, a priest, hears of Jeremiah's prophesy in the Valley of Hinnom. He doesn't like what he's hearing, probably because he was previously prophesying about peace.[22]

Then Pashhur beat Jeremiah the prophet, and put him in the stocks that were in the upper Benjamin Gate of the house of the Lord.

Jeremiah 20:2

The first time Jeremiah speaks is after Pashhur lets him out.[23] Through him, God gives Pashhur a personal message. God calls Pashhur "Terror on Every Side" and promises Pashhur will watch as his friends, family, and city are taken by the Babylonians. God was confirming the warning Jeremiah was relaying.

Pashhur's role mostly ends there. We don't see a confrontation, or more punishment to Jeremiah, and the chapter just moves on. However, what follows is likely directly related to this latest installment of persecution.

Cursed be the day
on which I was born!
The day when my mother bore me,
let it not be blessed!

Jeremiah 20:14

The transparency and honesty Jeremiah showed when sharing his struggles with God is a good reminder of the intimacy God wants with His children. God already knows what we're feeling, but being vulnerable and genuine is an important part of intimacy. Plus, consciously acknowledging feelings helps to move past them.

Jeremiah blames God for not protecting him. But God never promises to keep us from difficulty. Experiencing difficulty is part of how we grow closer to God. The better life is going the less we're willing to rely on God. It's when we have nothing left, when we're alone and miserable, that we are most willing turn back to our Father.

Jeremiah complains that God has deceived him, saying that his life is just a joke to those around him. Then he praises God for a verse or two, only to fall back into complaining.

Sin has a frustrating cyclical nature. We face difficulties with whining, tears, and foot stomping—until we realize we're not in control and look to God. When we feel His closeness again, we become complacent and start the cycle over again.

It's natural to be happy when things are going well and to be upset when things aren't. But relying on God requires a conscious decision. He doesn't ask us to have strength to get through everything. He has the strength, and if we ask, He will equip us.

Jeremiah 21

"Inquire of the Lord for us, for Nebuchadnezzar king of Babylon is making war against us. Perhaps the Lord will deal with us according to all his wonderful deeds and will make him withdraw from us."

Jeremiah 21:2

Babylon's army is now at the borders of Judah, and Zedekiah, king of Judah, asks Jeremiah to petition God to make the army withdraw. Zedekiah sends two priests to ask Jeremiah this question. (The name Pashhur comes up again, but this is a common name and it's believed to be a different person.[24]) Since Jeremiah's prophecies are starting to come true, he's being respected instead of despised.[25]

Zedekiah falls into a thought pattern that is alive and well today. He believes God will save them simply because they're heirs of Abraham. Despite God's persistent call to repentance, Zedekiah merely wants to "get rid of their trouble, not to make peace with God and be reconciled to him".[26]

So many people ask for prayers when times are tough, but still live their own way. It's easy to fall into the pattern of wanting God's help when something is wrong without truly following Him.

God doesn't blindside us with consequences. Like Judah, we get many opportunities to come to God and repent. We may still experience the consequences of the sin, but when we are relying on God we are able to learn through them. Repentance can be hard. We often say, "Hey God, I have this problem, please help me out of it!" instead of asking, "God, is my sin the cause of this? Is there something I need to change in my life?"

God doesn't loathe giving His protection. He wants to protect us. This doesn't mean stopping everything from happening, because what kind of life can a person have when you protect them from everything?

To truly walk with God under His protection, we have to be obedient. We can't just blissfully live in our sin, as Zedekiah did (and almost all of Judah for that matter) and expect God to bestow blessings and miracles.

> *"He who stays in this city shall die by the sword, by famine, and by pestilence, but he who goes out and surrenders to the Chaldeans who are besieging you shall live and shall have his life as a prize of war."*
>
> *Jeremiah 21:9*

God's response to Zedekiah's plea is they should surrender—they shouldn't even fight, but instead give themselves up immediately as captives. This is the only way they can survive.

Judah has spent generations using superficial rituals and words to fulfill their side of the covenant. Their security was in their pride as children of Abraham. God challenged that pride with a call to action that required true surrender.

Jeremiah 22

In the Bible, the books and chapters are not always in chronological order. Many go back and forth between seasons, even generations. "The prophecies of this book are not placed here in the same order in which they were preached".[27] It's helpful to be aware of whether or not the book you're reading is always chronological, sometimes chronological, or a compilation.

> *Thus says the Lord: "Go down to the house of the king of Judah and speak there this word...."*
>
> *Jeremiah 22:1*

In this flashback, God has an important message for the royal house of Judah, particularly Jehoahaz, mentioned as Shallum here; Jehoiakim, Jehoahaz's older brother; and Jehoiachin, Jehoiakim's son. These three men have committed sins that've put their royal line in jeopardy.

Jehoahaz has risen above his older brothers in line for the throne after his father died. Though this may not seem like an offense, the story of Esau and Jacob teaches us differently. Grabbing something promised instead of waiting for it to be bestowed is a failure to trust God. God promised He'd make Jacob great. However, as the youngest, Jacob felt—with some added worry from his mother—that he needed to trick and lie to become great. God simply wanted Jacob to trust Him.

We desire to control the outcomes of our lives. But in reality, no matter how much it may seem we're in control, we never are. We can't control the universe. In trying to manipulate and squirm our way to where we want to be, we distance ourselves from God.

Jehoahaz is told "he shall return here no more, but in the place where they have carried him captive, there shall he die, and he shall never see this land again" (Jeremiah 22:11-12). As it turns out, this becomes the fate of all three men, but for different reasons. Because of their wickedness they will die as captives in a foreign land.

Jehoiakim is consumed with pride. Though his father was wealthy, he was a good man. But unlike his father, Jehoiakim was greedy. He "builds [himself] a great house with spacious upper rooms" (Jeremiah 22:14). Jehoiakim likely didn't have the funds to do these upgrades and probably cheated his workers out of their wages.[28] The home he built was not just for his shelter but was a boastful sign of his greatness.

There is nothing inherently wrong with being rich or well off, but money has a natural pull towards sin. Though Josiah was royalty, he cared less about his possessions and more about helping his people back to God. Jehoiakim only wanted such a resplendent house to tower over others and legitimize his reign as king. When we flaunt our wealth and position instead of using it as a tool for God's glory, money becomes a false god.

Jehoiachin's specific sins aren't listed, except that he has refused to listen. He may not have been listening when his father and uncle were warned of their sins, or when all of Judah was warned of theirs. Whatever the case, he was stubborn and would not change.

The matter-of-fact description of their captures may sound like God enjoyed seeing it happen, but it surely grieved His heart to watch these men fail to change. They were of the line of David. They were descended of a man after God's own heart. They'd fallen so far.

We're only saved by our own admission of guilt and need for a savior. We don't get by because our parents were saved. We're each charged with knowing God and of submitting our lives to Him.

Our family lines can't save us, but the great news is, they also can't condemn us. Apart from Christ, we all stand condemned before God, as sinners from the line of Adam. When we're covered in Christ, we're no longer defined by the sin of Adam, nor ourselves, nor the sin of our earthly families.

Generations later, the Savior came from the line of David—a line that was fallen and broken because of sin and stubborn hearts was remade to save all men.

Jeremiah 23

"Both prophet and priest are ungodly;
even in my house I have found their evil,
declares the Lord...."

Jeremiah 23:11

God addresses the false prophets and priests directly. He has been watching, and He is brokenhearted by their actions.

As we've heard many times before, the prophets of Judah have been falsely teaching, promising Judah peace and good from God. The prophets go even further in their ungodliness. Not only were they telling lies they attributed to God—which in itself is bad enough—they were also living deceitfully sinful lives and hoping God wouldn't notice.

Though we know God is omniscient and omnipresent, sometimes we convince ourselves He won't see everything we do. Or we convince ourselves He won't care. The prophets were committing sinful acts in the temple and hoping to get away with them because they were His prophets. But God doesn't let people get away with things. He loves us too much and He is perfectly just.

The prophets and priests were pulling God's people away from Him, and this angered Him. They were giving out false information, driving a wedge between God and His chosen people. God does not take lightly those who shepherd His people away from Him. He reminds the prophets and priests that He's seen every one of their actions, and that nothing slips past Him.

But in the prophets of Jerusalem
I have seen a horrible thing:
they commit adultery and walk in lies;

they strengthen the hands of evildoers,
so that no one turns from his evil;
all of them have become like Sodom to me,
and its inhabitants like Gomorrah."

Jeremiah 23:14

Not all the blame falls on the prophets and priests. The people of Judah are still responsible for their actions, despite the false teaching. And while ancestors' success or failure at passing down godly precepts can help or hinder our walk with God, each person is accountable individually before Him.

God never stopped sending Judah true prophets, but they had to discern the truth. We have even less of an excuse today. We have the Holy Spirit dwelling in us, who will help us discern truth in what we hear.

God wasn't only warning the prophets and priests. He also offered a great hope. Before He starts warning the prophets and priests, God promises a special prophet, one who will be called "the Lord is our righteousness" (Jeremiah 23:6). This prophet is Jesus—the perfect shepherd who cares about the sheep as much as God does. Jesus came to lead people back to God and away from the false prophets that were rampant in His time and still are today.

God offers hope even in the midst of a reprimand. He doesn't want us to fall into the traps of the enemy or the ravages of sin. He gives us hope and a way back to Him, even in our darkest moments.

Jeremiah 24

God shows Jeremiah a vision of two fruit baskets, one good and one gone bad. The good fruit represents the exiles from Judah who were taken away to the land of the Chaldeans. Some exiles aren't mentioned in Jeremiah but are in other books of the Bible. Daniel and his friends make up some of that exile group, as does Ezekiel, another prophet.

> *"Thus says the Lord, the God of Israel: Like these good figs, so I will regard as good the exiles from Judah, whom I have sent away from this place to the land of the Chaldeans. I will set my eyes on them for good, and I will bring them back to this land. I will build them up, and not tear them down; I will plant them, and not pluck them up. I will give them a heart to know that I am the Lord, and they shall be my people and I will be their God, for they shall return to me with their whole heart."*
>
> *Jeremiah 24:5-7*

Though not all the exiles repented before they were sent away, it seems many may have been "shocked into repentance, and committed to the single-minded worship of God".[29] God used the exile for both His glory and Judah's good. We know that Daniel especially found great favor with the king of Babylon, Nebuchadnezzar. God used Daniel, through his unwavering faith, to speak to one of the greatest rulers of the era. Many times, we find ourselves in places that are uncomfortable. These are places we'd never put ourselves, but they're places where God can reach us more intimately than in any place we would choose for ourselves.

> *"But thus says the Lord: Like the bad figs that are so bad they cannot be eaten, so will I treat Zedekiah the king of Judah, his officials, the remnant of Jerusalem who remain in this*

*land, and those who dwell in the land of Egypt.... And I will
send sword, famine, and pestilence upon them, until they
shall be utterly destroyed from the land that I gave to them
and their fathers."*

Jeremiah 24:8,10

The second group, the bad fruit, have a very different future. These people won't find peace or security. They have forsaken their God and have been left to their consequences.

God sometimes allows us to suffer the consequences of our sin, so He can change and use us in awesome ways. Additionally, the consequences experienced by one person can light the path for another. God doesn't desire for anyone to suffer. God wants all hearts to turn back to Him, and sometimes He uses the consequences of those in unrepentance as a testimony for others.

God sent this vision to Jeremiah to remind him that God's ways are not our ways. We don't know how or when He'll use us in the lives of others. Our focus must be in trusting Him. He can and will use both the easy and difficult times to grow and use us, if we surrender our lives to Him.

Jeremiah 25

When I read, I tend to identify with the most virtuous character. But when I read the Bible, this tendency can obscure the truth. When I see myself as the person doing everything right, or even the person doing the right thing in a particular situation, I miss the chance to see where I can be growing.

I want to be like Jeremiah. I want to be the person God chooses to teach His people. I want to effortlessly avoid sin and help others to avoid it as well. But I know I've been just like Judah, entrenched in sin so deeply that I stubbornly refuse to blush.

Jeremiah and the other prophets before and after him have brought to the attention of Israel the need for repentance. They've begged God's chosen people to turn away from their sins and choose God again. His people have continually decided to stay where they are. They chose destruction over asking for forgiveness.

"And if they refuse to accept the cup from your hand to drink, then you shall say to them, 'Thus says the Lord of hosts: You must drink! For behold, I begin to work disaster at the city that is called by my name, and shall you go unpunished? You shall not go unpunished, for I am summoning a sword against all the inhabitants of the earth, declares the Lord of hosts.'"

Jeremiah 25:28-29

God gave Judah so many chances to come back to Him, and now they're being given the cup they've pressed to drink. He calls Nebuchadnezzar, the pagan king of Babylon, His servant over Judah. He sends Nebuchadnezzar to take Judah into captivity. God has declared servitude for His people yet again, because, yet again, they have walked away and are too stubborn to come back.

God didn't want to bring destruction on His people. He didn't want them to fall into captivity again. He wanted them to be free. But they weren't satisfied being a free people. They wanted to be like other nations. And in this world, to be like the world means being a captive.

The only true freedom is the freedom found in God. God asks us to be completely different from the world. Being made in the image of God, people share some common virtues, such as love, forgiveness, and compassion. But as Christ-followers we are motivated differently. When we lean on God, our virtues don't lead to burnout, they aren't limited in the number of times we can perform them, and they have nothing to do with what others do to us first.

The nation of Israel was meant to be a light in their world—a different type of nation and people, with a true God as their king. They chose to give up that identity to be like the other nations, and fought over which human was the rightful king, splitting the nation. Because they gave up their God-given identity, they also gave up the freedom God wanted to give them.

I always want to choose freedom. I want to be like Jeremiah and choose the one true God over any other. But I also know I have many of the same tendencies of Judah. Unless I learn from Judah and what God allowed to happen to them because of their sin, I may find myself stuck in their chains.

Jeremiah 26

Jeremiah has been nothing but faithful in delivering God's messages to His people, but that hasn't stopped them from persecuting him. Once more, Jeremiah prophesies and finds himself in a life or death situation. He warns Judah if they don't turn back, God will destroy Jerusalem and the temple. After he's finished delivering this prophecy, he's taken to the temple to stand trial in front of the officials of Judah.

> *Then the priests and the prophets said to the officials and to all the people, "This man deserves the sentence of death, because he has prophesied against this city, as you have heard with your own ears."*
>
> *Jeremiah 26:11*

There was no beating around the bush at this trial. Nobody present wanted to hear this message, even though it was from God. They continued to ignore similar prophesies from the past promising the same fate for Jerusalem if the people continued in their ways. The priests and prophets—who were not relaying God's messages, but their own—wanted to have Jeremiah killed.

King Jehoiakim already had another prophet, Uriah, killed for giving the same prophecy. Uriah fled to Egypt, but Jehoiakim had him hunted down and killed. Yet another prophet, Micah, whom Jeremiah quotes in his statement of defense, gave the same prophecy as well. But the king at the time, Hezekiah, didn't put him to death. One prophet lived and one died for the same message, and now Jeremiah is between these two fates.

Though most of us won't face death for speaking about God, we can face hostility, abandonment, and other consequences from people who didn't want to hear God's message. There will always be priests and prophets in our lives—people who are religious and are more educated, have a higher social status, or are better speakers than us. They may not want to hear God's truth because of deeply held beliefs. Despite this, we must strive to be obedient when God calls us to speak. It's one of the most important things we can do.

We will also have officials and people of the city in our lives. We may have peers who are not religious or who may be authorities to us, who hear God's message and are ambivalent. They listen but refuse to respond. They may believe they can't or may not want to change. We should continue to diligently listen for God's leading and obey when He moves us to speak.

Lastly, some people will listen and respond. They are hungry for God's message and His Word. They've been waiting to hear God speak. God doesn't need us to talk about Him. He wants us to share Him with the world. He does all the work—He changes hearts and calls people to Him, but He wants us to share in those moments.

Jeremiah knew that God was in charge. He didn't try to run when he was arrested. He didn't try to backpedal and talk his way out of a death sentence. He trusted that God's message was true and that whatever happened as a result of sharing it was part of God's plan. We don't know who will hear and receive His Word when we share it, but we can trust in His perfect plans.

Jeremiah 27

What a gracious God we serve! This thought was far from the first I had when I read this chapter. My first thought was, how can these people be so blind? But, as I pondered it for a bit, my heart shifted. I realized I'm often like Judah. I can be blind to struggles in my life that are obvious to others and look past God's grace. What makes me any different from Judah?

> *""...But any nation that will bring its neck under the yoke of the king of Babylon and serve him, I will leave on its own land, to work it and dwell there, declares the Lord. ""*
> *To Zedekiah king of Judah I spoke in like manner: "Bring your necks under the yoke of the king of Babylon, and serve him and his people and live."*
>
> *Jeremiah 27:11-12*

God's grace shows up in a big way. Zedekiah, the current king of Judah, is advised to surrender to the now invading Babylonians. This may not seem like a very gracious request, but God makes a special promise. If Judah surrenders, God promises they will stay in their lands instead of being taken away to Babylon.

God was actually making two promises. One, God wouldn't take the people from the land He gave them, and two, their punishment would be lightened. Instead of being refugees in a foreign land, they could stay in their own homes. They would still be ruled by Babylon but would avoid being at the bottom of the class system in another kingdom.

God had already "given all these lands into the hand of Nebuchadnezzar, the king of Babylon, [God's] servant" (Jeremiah 27:6). The land would belong to Babylon whether Judah fought or surrendered. Judah's choice was how they would live under Babylonian rule.

To say Nebuchadnezzar is God's servant is odd, but the truth is, even the worst of men can be used by God for His purposes—and usually in spite of themselves. "God calls [Nebuchadnezzar] his servant because He employed him as an instrument of his providence for the chastising of the nations, and particularly his own people." [30] God used Nebuchadnezzar's hubris for His purposes.

Judah's surrender was both to God and man—to man, they had to lose their nation, and to God, they had to confess and repent. In our lives, we fight for the independence to believe and desire as we will, without God. Our surrender is to submit to God's plan. The choice is still difficult. It's not easy to yield control to someone else. But, as we see with Judah and Babylon, sometimes God asks us to surrender so He can show us grace.

God could've let Nebuchadnezzar capture Judah immediately. But He gave Judah time to come to Him. God is so gracious with His timing; His timing is never wrong. God held back Nebuchadnezzar's troops to give Judah more time to repent.

Can you feel how much He wanted them to trust Him? To love Him? To serve Him? He feels just as strongly about us.

Jeremiah 28

Then the prophet Jeremiah spoke to Hananiah the prophet in the presence of the priests and all the people who were standing in the house of the Lord, and the prophet Jeremiah said, "Amen! May the Lord do so; may the Lord make the words that you have prophesied come true, and bring back to this place from Babylon the vessels of the house of the Lord, and all the exiles..."

Jeremiah 28:5-6

Jeremiah is confronted with a prophecy from Hananiah foretelling the triumph of Judah over Babylon in two years. Jeremiah knew this was too easy to be true.[31] Jeremiah cares deeply about his people, but he knows they must return to God to have any chance of peace. When he responds, he starts with a prayer for his people.

In the age of social media, when people are more ready than ever to say whatever pops into their head, this should be one of Jeremiah's greatest examples for us. We don't have to answer harshly. Ever. We can settle disputes calmly and confidently when we lean on God. We can use these moments to speak the truth into lives of people around us.

Directly after his prayer for peace, Jeremiah admonishes Hananiah and the others to challenge what they hear. He encourages them to compare their prophesies with proven historical prophesies.

Though Jesus doesn't walk among us today, we do have God's infallible Word. It's our faithful tool against which we can test everything. God will never contradict himself. His Word can be difficult to understand. But God is constant. Though times have changed, the truths of the Bible hold firm.

Hananiah continues to proclaim false prophesies and rips the yoke from Jeremiah's neck (which Jeremiah may have "carried as a memorial of what he had prophesied concerning the enslavement of the nations to Nebuchadnezzar"[32]), but Jeremiah doesn't take the bait. He "went his way" (Jeremiah 28:11).

We don't always have to have an answer. Sometimes we won't have something to say right away. It's okay to not respond or engage. We may feel stupid or inadequate, but that's not true. Those faithful to God don't put words into His mouth just to win an argument.

Jeremiah 29

Some correspondence takes place. First, Jeremiah writes to those who were taken to Babylon as exiles, sharing what God told him about their captivity. Then the false prophet Shemaiah writes to Judah, telling them to disregard Jeremiah's prophecy. Finally, Jeremiah responds to Shemaiah.

> *"Thus says the Lord of hosts, the God of Israel, to all the exiles whom I have sent into exile from Jerusalem to Babylon: Build houses and live in them; plant gardens and eat their produce. Take wives and have sons and daughters; take wives for your sons, and give your daughters in marriage, that they may bear sons and daughters; multiply there, and do not decrease. But seek the welfare of the city where I have sent you into exile, and pray to the Lord on its behalf, for in its welfare you will find your welfare."*
>
> *Jeremiah 29:4-7*

Judah is to be captive for seventy years. God tells them to make it their home. He tells them to do what they would do in Judah. He tells them to pray for Babylon, that it would prosper. As long as they're peaceful in Babylon they will prosper as well.

While Babylon was a literal reality for Judah, it echoes in our lives today. We often find ourselves in situations or places we didn't expect but may be in for a while. It may be for discipline, as it was for Judah, or it may be for some other part of His plan—but whatever the reason, God sends us for His glory. He wants us to rely on Him wherever we are.

Though their children might, the generation exiled in Babylon would never see home again. Like the generation of Israel that didn't get to see the Promised Land, God wanted them to be grateful for what He would do for them in Babylon, and to give the hope of home to their children. When we're joyful in difficult circumstances we show God's power and bring Him glory.

> *"Send to all the exiles, saying, 'Thus says the Lord concerning Shemaiah of Nehelam: Because Shemaiah had prophesied to you when I did not send him, and has made you trust in a lie, therefore thus says the Lord: Behold, I will punish Shemaiah of Nehelam and his descendants. He shall not have anyone living among this people, and he shall not see the good that I will do to my people, declares the Lord, for he has spoken rebellion against the Lord.'"*

Jeremiah 29:31-32

God punished Shemaiah for disregarding God's word. Shemaiah saw Jeremiah's prophecy fulfilled, but still called Jeremiah a false prophet and incited rebellion amongst Judah. "And, if vengeance shall be taken on those that rebel, much more on those that teach rebellion by their doctrine and example."[33]

God gave clear directions to Judah to have His protection while in captivity. He offers His companionship, strength, and wisdom in times of struggle. True joy in difficult circumstances can bring more glory to God than words ever could.

Jeremiah 30

"Thus says the Lord, the God of Israel: Write in a book all the words that I have spoken to you. For behold, days are coming, declares the Lord, when I will restore the fortunes of my people, Israel and Judah, says the Lord, and I will bring them back to the land that I gave to their fathers, and they shall take possession of it."

Jeremiah 30:2-3

One reason some scholars think God commanded Jeremiah to write this is so those who didn't respond initially could read it later and be moved.[34] It was also for future generations to see God's prophesies and their fulfillment.

God likens Judah's strife to the pain of childbirth. God used birth rather than death because, "it shall end in joy at last, and the pain…shall be forgotten".[35] He didn't see the pain Judah was experiencing as the outcome, He saw it as the pain of birthing something new. Often, difficulty is not a useless circumstance, but the pain of new life.

God can turn situations that seem hopeless and defeating into experiences that are strengthening and encouraging. When we rely on His strength instead of our own, He can turn our pain into something amazing.

"Behold, I will restore the fortunes of the tents of Jacob and have compassion on his dwellings; the city shall be rebuilt on its mound, and the palace shall stand where it used to be. Out of them shall come songs of thanksgiving, and the voices of those who celebrate. I will multiply them, and they shall not

be few; I will make them honored, and they shall not be small.
Their children shall be as they were of old, and their congre-
gations shall be established before me…"

God promises to rebuild Israel (including Judah) right where she fell. There will be songs of praise where there were once songs of lamentations. God will bring back the glory of Israel and she'll once again be His beautiful bride. But first, Israel must go through the discipline necessary to understand how worthy God is to be praised.

Sometimes God can feel very far away, especially when we're being disciplined or grown. Though He never moves away from His children, we might struggle to experience the emotional sense that He's close. As I fight through those feelings and commit to finding God in my present circumstances, I move closer to Him. We need to cherish those times for what they are: opportunities to love God—because in the end, He is who He promises He is.

Jeremiah 31

God gives Judah hope for the future, to help them be content in their present situation. God gives us glimpses of what we can hope for to help us be content in the present. Jeremiah has been encouraging Judah find contentment in their seventy year stay in Babylon.

> *"Behold, the days are coming, declares the Lord, when I will sow the house of Israel and the house of Judah with the seed of man and the seed of beast. And it shall come to pass that as I have watched over them to pluck up and break down, to overthrow, destroy, and bring harm, so I will watch over them to build and to plant, declares the Lord."*
>
> *Jeremiah 31:27-28*

God disciplines us because He loves us. He corrects us so we grow. God doesn't take joy in our suffering, otherwise He wouldn't have sent His Son to die—in one of the most painful ways possible—to spare us from the penalty of sin. He wants us to be planting and building with Him, not destroyed and overthrown.

When someone we care about comes close to harm, we may have a strong reaction. A parent might react by yanking back a child straying too close to a road. The parent's concern causes them to react quickly. As we've seen in His patience with Judah, God doesn't react emotionally, seeking retribution, but He does take strong action when necessary. He knows the benefits to the pain of His discipline. His discipline has eternal effects.

> *"Behold, the days are coming, declares the Lord, when I will make a new covenant with the house of Israel and the house of Judah, not like the covenant that I made with their fathers*

74

on the day when I took them by the hand to bring them out of
the land of Egypt, my covenant that they broke, though I was
their husband, declares the Lord. For this is the covenant that
I will make with the house of Israel after those days, declares
the Lord: I will put my law within them, and I will write it
on their hearts. And I will be their God, and they shall be my
people.... For I will forgive their iniquity, and I will remember
their sin no more."

Jeremiah 31:31-34

God gives Judah the greatest hope—the hope of the Messiah: "...for Christ came not to destroy the law, but to fulfill it; but the law shall be written in their hearts by the finger of the Spirit as formerly it was written in the tablets of stone."[36] The law of God would become indwelling. "God writes his law in the hearts of all believers, makes it ready and familiar to them, at hand when they have occasion to use it...."[37]

There is always hope for our future when Christ is our hope. We can have joy in long-suffering times because God is with us. We can have joy in bright, shining days, because God is with us. God will never forsake us. His love is enduring. We never have to be without His joy.

Jeremiah 32

Jeremiah is approached by his cousin to buy a piece of land that is his to redeem. Jeremiah knows he should accept this offer, because God told him his cousin would approach him with such a proposition. At the time, not only is Jeremiah currently under arrest, and therefore completely unable to use the land, but Judah is almost entirely captured and destroyed. It probably seemed like a silly thing to do, but Jeremiah still obeyed because "he has learnt…to recognize the hidden hand of God in what befalls him".[38]

Opportunities that seem small to us are often the ones God uses in big ways. Buying a flower or a coffee for someone may seem like a small act of service, but it may have a big impact on that person's life. We can't usually see the larger picture.

I love to embroider, but my favorite part isn't the side with the picture, it's the back full of messy bunches of thread. It's the beauty of the color and blur and knowing this giant mess makes a beautiful picture. It's the same with life. I get to see the messy blur of color, but I know that I trust in a God who sees the picture the mess makes. God knows exactly what people need, and if we obey Him when He places something on our heart, we can play a part in His plans.

Jeremiah doesn't just purchase the land and then grumble silently to himself or speculate about the purpose. He immediately takes his question to God. Jeremiah praises God for His power to do the impossible, and for the works He's already done for His people. He then brings up his concern that though the Chaldeans have brought almost complete destruction, "you, O Lord God, have said to me, 'Buy the field for money and get witnesses'" (Jeremiah 32:25).

Notice that Jeremiah started out his prayer with praise—reminding himself and thanking God for all that God had already done. He wasn't accusing God of doing something foolish. Instead, he was asking God for clarity to better understand what God was doing. He came with curiosity, not suspicion.

God answers Jeremiah's question, but before He does, He reminds Jeremiah why Judah is suffering. I doubt Jeremiah needed much of a reminder of this anymore—but God repeats himself for a reason. "Jeremiah knew not how to sing both of mercy and judgement, but God here teaches to sing unto him of both. When we know not how to reconcile one word of God with another, we may yet be sure that both are true, both are pure, both shall be made good, and not one iota or tittle of either shall fall to the ground."[39]

After He reminds Jeremiah of Judah's sins, consequences, and future hope, God simply tells Jeremiah, "fields shall be bought in this land of which you are saying, 'It is a desolation...'" (Jeremiah 32:43) and that He "will restore their fortunes" (Jeremiah 32:44). God promises though this land seems worthless now, one day it will be highly valuable. God will restore and increase the worth of that land to bless His children in Judah.

Our lives can seem worthless at times, as though we've spent all our time and energy on things that left us empty. But God can restore us and make our lives worth more than we ever could on our own. And more than that, He desires to do this! He wants to take of our lives the pieces we consider worthless and turn them into priceless testimonies for His glory.

Jeremiah 33

The word of the Lord came to Jeremiah a second time, while
he was still shut up in the court of the guard: "Thus says the
Lord who made the earth, the Lord who formed it to establish
it—the Lord is his name: Call to me and I will answer you, and
will tell you great and hidden things that you have not known."

Jeremiah 33:1-3

We, as a very stubborn people, "are not only so disobedient that we
have need of precept upon precept to bring us to our duty, but so distrust-
ful that we have need of promise upon promise to bring us to our comfort".[40] Brushing aside God's insistence for a change in one's life is all too
natural. It often takes reminders from God, before we listen. Our hearts
need to be softened before we are willing to admit our need for change.

Judah is suffering because they refused to heed God's insistence for
their repentance. Their land is now a "place that is waste, without man
or beast." (Jeremiah 33:12) But God was still working on the hearts of
the people of Judah. They may have only been at the beginning of their
consequence, but God was far from giving up on them.

"... in all of its cities, there shall again be habitations of shep-
herds resting their flocks. In the cities of the hill country, in
the cities of the Shephelah, and in the cities of the Negeb, in
the land of Benjamin, the places about Jerusalem, and in the
cities of Judah, flocks shall again pass under the hands of the
one who counts them, says the Lord."

Jeremiah 33:12-13

God makes the people of Judah multiple promises for life after captivity. They'll again have herds and flocks, homes and cities, and mul-

tiplied and filled lands. These promises are repeated over and over to help them sink in.

Judah was anything but insignificant to God, even in their captivity. I imagine His description to Jeremiah was powerful and emotional. He was excited for His people's return! He didn't want them to remain stuck where they were. He wanted them to be able to rise above and come back into the promises He'd set out for them from the beginning.

God wanted Judah to know that the greatest fulfillment of His promises would come in the form of the Messiah, "a righteous Branch to spring up for David" who would "execute justice and righteousness in the land. In those days Judah will be saved, and Jerusalem will dwell securely..." (Jeremiah 33:15-16). Jesus would bring the ultimate restoration for which God's people longed.

We, as His children, need reminders of these promises because we have a hard time seeing the big picture and seeing how God's discipline leads to something wonderful. But God sees it. He already knows what we can and will have and be. And I truly believe He loves reminding us of how special and powerful those promises are.

Jeremiah 34

"Thus says the Lord, the God of Israel: Go and speak to Zedekiah king of Judah and say to him, 'Thus says the Lord: Behold, I am giving this city into the hand of the king of Babylon, and he shall burn it with fire.'"

Jeremiah 34:2

The prophecy Jeremiah delivers to Zedekiah takes place before Jeremiah is imprisoned. Jeremiah tells Zedekiah he'll be taken captive by Nebuchadnezzar, and the whole city will be burned. However, during this prophecy of destruction and captivity, God makes an unusual promise. He promises that Zedekiah will not die from the sword, but instead will die from natural causes. He also promises that he'll be missed and honored after his death.

Zedekiah didn't repent while he was king, but that doesn't mean he couldn't repent later. Sometimes it's during our consequences that we return to God. Some people come to Him because of difficulty, others because of wonderful events. Every person goes through different experiences. God knows what will specifically change each person's heart.

The word that came to Jeremiah from the Lord, after King Zedekiah had made a covenant with all the people in Jerusalem to make a proclamation of liberty to them, that everyone should set free his Hebrew slaves, male and female, so that no one should enslave a Jew, his brother.

Jeremiah 34:8-9

God was very pleased by this. He'd commanded any Jewish person who'd taken another Jewish person for a slave would release their slave in the seventh year. Judah had been ignoring this practice, but there was, finally, a movement to pick it up again.

At first, everyone freed their Hebrew slaves, potentially due to "the pinch of famine and the inconvenience of having many mouths to feed,"[41] "but afterward they turned around and took back the male and female slaves they had set free, and brought them into subjection as slaves." (Jeremiah 34:11).

God was angered by this quick backslide. Since His people took away the freedom of their brothers and sisters, God promises to take away their freedom as well. He promises "the men who transgressed my covenant...[will be] like the calf they cut in two..." (Jeremiah 34:18). Those who broke His covenant will suffer, in this case, enduring a death like that of their animal sacrifices.

Keeping promises is hard. Sometimes we agree to things before thinking them through, or we take on too much, or we agree when we are in a certain mood but later no longer feel that way. Each time we agree to something and then back out, our word is worth a little less. God wasn't surprised by Judah's reversal. God isn't surprised by anything, but Judah also had a bad reputation for saying and doing things they didn't intend to follow through on.

Words are important. I want my words, as well as my actions, to bring glory to God. If I speak flippantly, how can my word hold any weight? And if my word holds no weight, what good is my word about what God's done? People should be able to take me at my word. But most importantly, I want God to be able to take me at my word. I want my promises to Him to reflect His promises to me.

Jeremiah 35

During Jehoiakim's rein, after the Babylonian army had invaded, God sent Jeremiah to the Rechabites, a people that descended from Hobab, Moses's father-in-law. The Rechabites traveled with the Israelites, without ever becoming part of them. They "saw themselves as living witnesses to the pilgrim origins of Israel".[42] The Rechabites drank "no wine all [of their] days...[and] lived in tents..." (Jeremiah 35:8-9), but once the Babylonian army began invading Judah, they moved into Jerusalem to be safe.

God sends Jeremiah to the Rechabites with a large amount of wine. He has Jeremiah set the wine out and offer it to them. They steadfastly refuse, reminding Jeremiah it's against the father of their people to drink wine. It's strange that God has Jeremiah suggest these strict people break their laws, but God had a reason.

God was teaching Judah a lesson. "The Rechabites were obedient to one who was but a man like themselves, who had but the wisdom and power of a man, and was only the father of their flesh; but the Jews were disobedient to an infinite and eternal God, who had an absolute authority over them, as the Father of their spirits".[43]

I'm a rule follower, to a fault. I tie myself to man-made laws to the point where I have difficulty getting myself to cross the street where there isn't a crosswalk, because it's technically against the law.

Laws aren't inherently good or evil. But the point God was making wasn't about the moral alignment of laws. The point was we're usually so much better at following rules made by people than following rules made by God, even though He knows every one of us better than we know ourselves. He wants the best for us. He gave His Son so we could have abundant life. Yet, we find it difficult to obey His rules. It breaks my heart that I've found God's rules so easy to forget, and man's rules so easy to follow.

The command that Jonadab the son of Rechab gave to his sons, to drink no wine, has been kept, and they drink none to this day, for they have obeyed their father's command. I have spoken to you persistently, but you have not listened to me.... The sons of Jonadab the son of Rechab have kept the command that their father gave them, but this people has not obeyed me.

Jeremiah 35:14-16

God wasn't quiet. He wasn't hard to figure out. He literally wrote down His commandments for His people and sent prophet after prophet, and a whole tribe of priests to guide them, but still they refused to listen and decided to follow their own rules.

God promises the Rechabites they'll "never lack a man to stand before [Him]" (Jeremiah 35:19). He rewards their ability to be faithful. And He also promises to "[bring] upon Judah and all the inhabitants of Jerusalem all the disaster that [He had] pronounced against them" (Jeremiah 35:17). Judah received a promise of doom because they wouldn't commit to their heavenly, eternal father, while those who lived among them for generations diligently held fast to an earthly father.

Jeremiah 36

"Take a scroll and write on it all the words that I have spoken to you against Israel and Judah and all the nations, from the day I spoke to you, from the days of Josiah until today. It may be that the house of Judah will hear all the disaster that I intend to do to them, so that every one may turn from his evil way, and that I may forgive their iniquity and their sin."

Jeremiah 36:2-3

Jeremiah was a great speaker, but perhaps was not skilled at writing. He enlisted the help of Baruch, a scribe, to carry out this command.[44]

Either it took a long time to write all these prophecies down, or Jeremiah and Baruch waited intentionally before presenting the scroll to the princes at the temple. Whatever the case, Jeremiah received the command to write the scroll in Jehoiakim's fourth year of reign, but it wasn't read to the princes until his fifth. And since Jeremiah was banned from the temple, he sent Baruch to read the scroll.

The scroll is read during the days of Judah's fasting. Fasting is a religious act that, when used as intended, brings us closer to God. Through fasting, we forsake the ephemeral satisfaction of this world so we can more clearly see our need for God. In their refusal to heed God's call for repentance, Judah's fasts were wasted. Their fasting was nothing but a physical action, disconnected from any spiritual significance.

Even as Judah mocked His commands by participating in meaningless fasts, God still gave them a chance to repent. He wants to reconcile His people to himself.

So they went into the court to the king, having put the scroll in the chamber of Elishama the secretary, and they reported all the words to the king. Then the king sent Jehudi to get the

scroll, and he took it from the chamber of Elishama the secre-
tary. And Jehudi read it to the king and all the officials who
stood beside the king. It was the ninth month, and the king was
sitting in the winter house, and there was a fire burning in the
fire pot before him. As Jehudi read three or four columns, the
king would cut them off with a knife and throw them into the
fire in the fire pot, until the entire scroll was consumed in the
fire that was in the fire pot.

Jeremiah 36:20-23

God sees Jehoiakim's heart and through Jeremiah tells him He
knows Jehoiakim burned the scroll because it prophesied that "the king
of Babylon will certainly come and destroy this land, and will cut off
from it man and beast." (Jeremiah 36:29) Jehoiakim's heart was hardened
against God's punishment, despite him having already seen some of the
destruction of which God had spoken—Babylon's king had already come
and destroyed some of the lands of Judah in his third year of reign.

We all have the chance to respond to the truth—either in the way
Jehoiakim responded when he got angry and refused to listen to God, or
in the way Jeremiah responded when he acted on God's words.

Jeremiah 37

Zedekiah the son of Josiah, whom Nebuchadnezzar king of Babylon made king in the land of Judah, reigned instead of Coniah the son of Jehoiakim. But neither he nor his servants nor the people of the land listened to the words of the Lord that he spoke through Jeremiah the prophet.

Jeremiah 37:1-2

Zedekiah asks Jeremiah to pray for peace for the country and protection from the Chaldeans. The Chaldeans have been fought off by Judah with some help from the Egyptian army, but now the Egyptians are leaving. Jeremiah refuses to pray, and instead prophesies the Chaldeans will return to burn the city. He promises that "even if [Judah] should defeat the whole army of the Chaldeans...and there remained of them only wounded men...they would rise up and burn this city with fire." (Jeremiah 37:10)

God has already, very clearly, told Judah what they must do to prevent these disasters from befalling their city. He hasn't left them in the dark, wondering how they can avert it. But they don't want to change. They want to continue living the same way they have and still be saved.

After refusing to pray for peace, Jeremiah joins the crowds leaving Jerusalem. As he's leaving the city, a guard, "Irijah the son of Shelemiah, son of Hananiah seized Jeremiah the prophet, saying 'You are deserting to the Chaldeans'" (Jeremiah 37:13). It's speculated that the Hananiah listed as Irijah's grandfather, was one of the false prophets that Jeremiah spoke out against. If so, he was probably looking for a reason to legally arrest Jeremiah—and could do so by claiming he was leaving the city to join the Chaldeans.[45]

When Jeremiah had come to the dungeon cells and remained there many days, King Zedekiah sent for him and received him. The king questioned him secretly in his house and said, "Is there any word from the Lord?" Jeremiah said, "There is." Then he said, "You shall be delivered into the hand of the king of Babylon."

Jeremiah 37:16-17

Though this is very bad news to the king, and would probably anger him, "Jeremiah was one that had obtained mercy of the Lord to be faithful, and would not, to obtain mercy of man, be unfaithful either to God or to his prince; he therefore tells him the truth, the whole truth".[46]

We can't bend the truth to avoid tough situations. As followers of Christ, it's much more important to be faithful to Him than to please any person.

God works Jeremiah's faithfulness for Jeremiah's good. After telling the king his fate, Jeremiah begs not to be sent back to prison. Though odd, King Zedekiah grants him permission to stay in "the court of the guard," (Jeremiah 37:21) a courtyard in the palace used as housing for prisoners.

As Christians, we have nothing to fear. Though Jeremiah begged to be moved "lest [he] die" (Jeremiah 37:20) in the house of the secretary, he was willing to die for God's glory if that was God's will.[47] Though we face times when hard truths will test relationships beyond their breaking points, we must be ready. Though we may face pain and torment while making disciples, we must be ready. God is in control, and we're called to be faithful to Him.

Jeremiah 38

Jeremiah tells the remaining Israelites to "go out to the Chaldeans [to] live" (Jeremiah 38:2), meaning anyone who willingly gives themselves up will be spared the horrors of war. The princes of Judah accuse Jeremiah of "weakening the hands of the soldiers who are left in this city, and the hands of all the people, by speaking such words to them." (Jeremiah 38:4).

With the permission of the king of Judah, the princes threw Jeremiah in an old well, knowing he'd die a terrible death that people couldn't necessarily pin on them.[48] God's truths can be freeing to some, and scary to others. The princes feared the truth, and therefore attempted to bury it with Jeremiah. But God had another plan for him.

> *When Ebed-melech the Ethiopian, a eunuch who was in the king's house, heard that they had put Jeremiah into the cistern—the king was sitting in the Benjamin Gate— Ebed-melech went from the king's house and said to the king, "My lord the king, these men have done evil in all that they did to Jeremiah the prophet by casting him into the cistern, and he will die there of hunger, for there is no bread left in the city."*
>
> Jeremiah 38:7-9

This was a bold move for Ebed-melech, and nothing required him to risk anything for Jeremiah. He was calling out the king in front of a large crowd that included the men who threw Jeremiah into the well to begin with.[49] Ebed-melech's bravery is rewarded, and he succeeds in saving Jeremiah from the well. But he goes above and beyond obtaining Jeremiah's release. He physically frees Jeremiah himself, and with great care.

So Ebed-melech took the men with him and went to the house of the king, to a wardrobe in the storehouse, and took from there old rags and worn-out clothes, which he let down to Jeremiah in the cistern by ropes. Then Ebed-melech the Ethiopian said to Jeremiah, "Put the rags and clothes between your armpits and the ropes." Jeremiah did so.

Jeremiah 38:11-12

After his release, Jeremiah is called by the king once again, in hopes that God has a different word to give him.[50] But God, being constant as He is, tells him again to surrender. So often we can hear the word of God clearly, but because we want it to be something else, we keep asking. We keep hoping God will change His mind.

The king refuses to listen to Jeremiah, yet again, and ends up with the latter. He refuses even after Jeremiah tells him how poorly his choice would affect not only his city but his own family. The king decides that a slight chance at ridicule, since God promised that the Jews already in Babylon wouldn't kill him, is much worse than his city being burned to the ground and his family becoming prisoners of Babylon.

We cannot choose our consequences, but we can choose to obey. The king refused to obey God despite being told the path to take and the consequences should he not take it. Ebed-melech chose to care for a messenger of God without being told even once.

God's will is always done, whether we're willing or unwilling to participate obediently. Sometimes that means we miss out on wonderful opportunities, and sometimes it means we end up with terrible consequences.

Jeremiah 39

The history of Jerusalem as a free city ends. Though it appears to take them several months to do so, Nebuchadnezzar's army finally breaches Jerusalem's gates.

As soon as Babylon begins to take the city, Zedekiah realizes he needs to get out. He and his soldiers "[flee], going out of the city at night by way of the king's garden" (Jeremiah 39:4). But Zedekiah missed his chance for peace when he refused to listen to God's word through Jeremiah. He's taken captive by the Chaldean army and given a sentence worse than death.

> *The king of Babylon slaughtered the sons of Zedekiah at Riblah before his eyes, and the king of Babylon slaughtered all the nobles of Judah. He put out the eyes of Zedekiah and bound him in chains to take him to Babylon.*
>
> *Jeremiah 39:6-7*

Many innocent people were killed as the result of Zedekiah's choices. Not just his family and the nobles of Judah, but all the people of Jerusalem who fought against Babylon. Only Jeremiah, Ebed-melech, the poor of Jerusalem, and those they took captive were spared. The king of Babylon allowed the poor, who likely didn't fight, [51] to not only stay in the city, but he also gave them vineyards and fields.

The poor had better living conditions under Babylon than they had under the kings of Judah. "The rich had been proud oppressors, and now they were justly punished for their injustice; the poor had been patient sufferers, and now they were graciously awarded for their patience and amends made them for all their losses; for verily there is a God that judges in the earth, even in this world, much more in the other." [52] Sometimes God uses unlikely people to care for those no one else will.

Nebuchadnezzar king of Babylon gave command concerning Jeremiah through Nebuzaradan, the captain of the guard, saying, "Take him, look after him well, and do him no harm, but deal with him as he tells you." ... They entrusted him to Gedaliah the son of Ahikam, son of Shaphan, that he should take him home. So he lived among the people.

Jeremiah 39:11-12, 14

Before Jeremiah is rescued, God promises to also rescue Ebed-melech. "God, in recompensing men's services, has an eye to the principle they go upon in those services, and rewards according to those principles; and there is no principle of obedience that will be more acceptable to God, nor have a greater influence upon us, than a believing confidence in God".[53] Acts of kindness that come from faith in God have a greater intention than those motivated by other reasons.

God values action motivated by faith. Faith-motivated service usually requires us to leave our comfort zones, which in turn requires us to lean on Him. When we allow ourselves to be stretched in this way, we bring glory to God. Ebed-melech had to take bold action, action that was surely not comfortable, and this brought glory to God. His obedience kept God's messenger alive, and so he was rewarded with his own life during great turmoil.

Jeremiah 40

The next two chapters are the detailed story of Jeremiah's capture by the Chaldeans mentioned in the previous chapter, despite beginning with "the word that came from the Lord" (Jeremiah 40:1). The prophesy will come in chapter 42.

> *"Now, behold, I release you today from the chains on your hands. If it seems good to you to come with me to Babylon, come, and I will look after you well, but if it seems wrong to you to come with me to Babylon, do not come. See, the whole land is before you; go wherever you think it good and right to go. If you remain, then return to Gedaliah the son of Ahikam, son of Shaphan, whom the king of Babylon appointed governor of the cities of Judah, and dwell with him among the people. Or go wherever you think it right to go." So the captain of the guard gave him an allowance of food and a present, and let him go.*
>
> *Jeremiah 40:4-5*

Nebuzaradan doesn't force Jeremiah to accompany him. Rather he encourages him to go to Gedaliah. Gedaliah was the Jewish governor, appointed by the king of Babylon over those left in Judah. Though Nebuzaradan encourages Jeremiah to go back home, he doesn't force that on him either. Instead, he leaves him with food and probably money or clothes and allows him time to decide. This must have been a relief for Jeremiah, who "lately was tossed from one prison to another [and] may now walk at liberty from one possession to another".[54]

Allowing others to make their own choices can be frustrating, especially when they ignore sound advice. But we must not take responsibil ity for another's choices. We are responsible to God to speak truth and encourage others as He leads us. If we push others into what we think is best, we prevent them from owning their choice.

Jeremiah chooses to return to Judah and to the house of Gedaliah, where he finds trouble brewing. Gedaliah had pledged to protect the remaining Judeans and was already well-loved. People who had left Judah previously even returned to live under his rule.

Baalis, the king of the Ammonites, had a problem with Gedaliah. He "had a particular spite at Gedaliah…either out of malice to the nation of the Jew…or a personal pique against Gedaliah."[55] He employed Ishmael, from the line of David, to kill Gedaliah.

> *Then Johanan the son of Kareah spoke secretly to Gedaliah at Mizpah, "Please let me go and strike down Ishmael the son of Nethaniah, and no one will know it. Why should he take your life, so that all the Judeans who are gathered about you would be scattered, and the remnant of Judah would perish?" But Gedaliah the son of Ahikam said to Johanan the son of Kareah, "You shall not do this thing, for you are speaking falsely of Ishmael."*
>
> *Jeremiah 40:15-16*

Johanan wanted Gedaliah to let him kill Ishmael to prevent Ishmael killing Gedaliah, but to his credit, Gedaliah refused. "Herein he showed more courage and zeal than sense of justice; for, if it be lawful to kill for prevention, who then can be safe, since malice always suspects the worst?"[56]

How often do we support conclusions about someone, simply because we have something against them? Or worse, because we want to be liked ourselves? Avoiding gossip or taking a stand against hurtful things others say may attract ridicule, even from our friends. But we must be attentive to what comes out of our mouths as well as what we agree with from the mouths of others—even if the gossip is true. None of us deserve God's grace, and yet all of us, regardless of our offense, are invited to experience that free pardon in Christ.

Jeremiah 41

Ishmael gathers with Gedaliah and ten other men to break bread together. As they do so, "[they] rose up and struck down Gedaliah" (Jeremiah 41:2). They also took the time to kill anyone around who could've taken revenge on them.

The next day, a group of eighty men from the kingdom of Israel making their way to Jerusalem to mourn the loss of the temple pass near Mizpah. Ishmael meets this group, pretending to be in mourning as well, and murders seventy of them. Ten escape by begging for their lives to be spared in exchange for "stores of wheat, barley, oil, and honey hidden in the fields" (Jeremiah 41:8). Ishmael agrees, and takes them with the rest of his captives and plunder on his way to the Ammonites.

Consider Gedaliah's attitude and actions before his death. He's already been warned of Ishmael's desire to kill him by Johanan, which he dismissed. Despite this warning from a trustworthy source, he dines without guard with Ishmael, the very man about whom he was warned. Gedaliah had access to an army that scared Ishmael, and yet he went alone. He could've very easily prevented his own death if he'd only listened to his council and taken precautions.

As we actively live out being God's hands and feet, we must also remember that we live in a sin-ridden world. Taking unnecessary risks reflects poorly on God. He doesn't call us to be reckless for the fun of it, He calls us to live for His glory. This may mean doing things that seem reckless, such as selling your possessions and moving to a closed country to share the Gospel. Taking a moment to ask God for wisdom and discernment will help us see the path God is asking us to take.

Ishmael's actions were even more reckless. After killing Gedaliah, he goes out of the city and lures to their death, for no apparent reason, seventy men who simply came to mourn the temple. Ishmael, a man of royal blood, goes on a killing spree against his own people.

This is what happens when we allow sin to take over in our lives. We don't take precautions and suddenly one seemingly little sin spirals into many. In opening our hearts to one sin, it becomes that much easier to justify the next and then the next. We need to stay alert not just to the malice of others, but equally or more to our own evil tendencies.

We can't honor God by attempting to get close to worldly living. Choosing God requires our obedience so that we can reflect Him. When we do this, it's easier to share the Gospel, because it is evidently part of us, rather than something we are trying to sell.

Jeremiah 42

Though Jeremiah chose to live with Gedaliah in his home, he somehow does not become involved in Gedaliah's mess. Having already hidden and saved Jeremiah from seemingly impossible circumstances, God has proved more than faithful.[57]

Johanan and his men are set on heading to Egypt, and they're fearful of what the king of Babylon will do to them. Despite this, they still ask God what they should do.

> *Then they said to Jeremiah, "May the Lord be a true and faithful witness against us if we do not act according to all the word with which the Lord your God sends you to us. Whether it is good or bad, we will obey the voice of the Lord our God to whom we are sending you, that it may be well with us when we obey the voice of the Lord our God."*
>
> *Jeremiah 42:5-6*

Growing up in a Christian home, I heard often that I should ask God what to do, but I wasn't taught or showed what that would look like. I spent years asking God what I should do, while allowing my desired answer to linger in the back of my mind. Instead of asking for God's will and the peace to follow it, I hoped that God would go along with my will—thereby justifying my desires. These men had the same mindset. They didn't want to trust God, they wanted "to know if God [would] approve of their plan to migrate to Egypt".[58]

God waits ten days to give Johanan and his men an answer. When He does answer them, He tells them He knows they've already refused His will. God knows our hearts better than we do, and so does not need to answer us immediately. Sometimes we need time before we're ready to trust Him. Sometimes we need time to understand our feelings

Sometimes He's already told us what to do and we refused to listen. Whatever the case, the wait is an opportunity to grow in our trust in God.

> *"Do not fear the king of Babylon, of whom you are afraid. Do not fear him, declares the Lord, for I am with you, to save you and to deliver you from his hand. I will grant you mercy, that he may have mercy on you and let you remain in your own land. ... Thus says the Lord of hosts, the God of Israel: If you set your faces to enter Egypt and go to live there, then the sword that you fear shall overtake you there in the land of Egypt, and the famine of which you are afraid shall follow close after you to Egypt, and there you shall die."*
>
> *Jeremiah 42:11-12, 15-16*

Johanan and his men let fear of the king of Babylon overcome their desire to know God's will. God warns against fear often in the Bible, because fear is an intense motivator. It causes us to do things hastily. It makes us desperate. These are anxieties that waiting can fight. When we wait on God, we have time to think and consider other options. When we wait on God, we don't make quick decisions. When we wait on God, we get His best. When we truly wait on Him and are open to His will, we get all of Him instead of only what we're willing to let in. Waiting on God brings freedom from fear.

When we ask with truly open minds and hearts, instead of hoping that His answer will line up with ours, we can join with God in life-changing areas of service. We'll find that sometimes He asks us to do difficult things, but He'll never force us to do them. God asks for our trust, because He knows best, even when our immediate circumstances are difficult.

Jeremiah 43

God already knows Johanan won't follow through on his word. As Johanan hears this, he and his men accuse Jeremiah of lying.

> *"You are telling a lie. The Lord our God did not send you to say, 'Do not go to Egypt to live there,' but Baruch the son of Neriah has set you against us, to deliver us into the hand of the Chaldeans, that they may kill us or take us into exile in Babylon."*
>
> Jeremiah 43:2-3

So, they forcibly take Jeremiah and his scribe, Baruch, to Egypt. It seems that Johanan and his men "had regarded God as a power to enlist, not a lord to obey".[59]

That hits me right in the gut. How many times have I, too, viewed God in that way? Sometimes we ask God for His answer, but really only want a specific answer—an answer that is from our will, not His.

It's strange that Johanan and his men would take with them people whom they believe lied to them. Perhaps they thought that having a prophet in tow they could claim—either to themselves or anyone else—that they're still following God's word [60] and have the best understanding of God.[61]

But God is not a tool for man to wield at will. He goes with Jeremiah and sends a new message to Johanan and his men. God has Jeremiah "take great stones, such as are used for foundations, and lay them in the clay of furnace, or brick-kiln, which is in the open way, or beside the way that leads to Pharaoh's house".[62] He then tells Jeremiah to speak over the stones. "Thus says the Lord of hosts, the God of Israel: Behold, I will send and take Nebuchadnezzar the king of Babylon, my servant, and I will set his throne above these stones that I have hidden, and he will spread his royal canopy over them." (Jeremiah 43:10). Johanan and his men haven't brought desolation and death on only themselves, but now upon Egypt as well.

When I come across parts of the Bible that convey painful truths, I have a choice. I can ignore it with a justification that suits me, or I can wrestle with it, trusting that God's plan is perfect. There are parts of me that want God to be soft and hate death and destruction. But if there's one thing the book of Jeremiah shows us, it's that God is justice. Sometimes justice means death and destruction. But the beauty in that is His justice makes His mercy profound.

Just as Johanan and his men doomed the Egyptians by dismissing God's word and refusing to listen to it, we can do a disservice to many by not responding to God's word when we hear it in our own lives. We must wrestle through fear and be willing to step out in faith.

Jeremiah 44

As for the word that you have spoken to us in the name of the Lord, we will not listen to you.

Jeremiah 44:16

As I read these words, I hear my own heart. I hear the part of my heart that wants to stay angry, or the part that wants to watch this or listen to that because it's funny. I hear the part of my heart that doesn't want to risk messing up a friendship by telling someone a hard truth.

My heart is fickle, as is the heart of every human. It's part of our sinful nature. My heart so desires to do what God asks of me and to follow His word to the letter, but it also desires to wander. This is a constant battle; one I don't see an end to until I reach heaven.

But I don't believe for a second that there's any reason to give in. If ever there was a battle worth fighting, it's the one over my heart. Our spiritual battles do not happen in isolation. They affect those to whom God has asked me to minister.

Jeremiah addresses those in Judah insisting it's been "since [they] left off making offerings to the queen of heaven and pouring out drink offerings to her, [that they] have lacked everything and have been consumed by the sword and famine." (Jeremiah 44:18) But Jeremiah rebukes them and reminds them of the real reason they have been suffering.

The Lord could no longer bear your evil deeds and the abominations that you committed. Therefore your land has become a desolation and a waste and a curse without inhabitant, as it is this day. It is because you made offerings and because you

sinned against the Lord and did not obey the voice of the Lord
or walk in his law and in his statutes and in his testimonies
that this disaster has happened to you, as at this day.

Jeremiah 44:22-23

I commend Jeremiah for his patience with these people. How many times, in how many years, has he spoken to these same people about their idolatry causing their destruction? And yet, they're still trying to find answers and fulfillment outside of God.

All they had to do was repent. God wanted Judah back, and was calling them repeatedly to return to Him, but they refused. They sought answers from every other possible source. They fled to Egypt for protection under Pharaoh. They were absolutely dead set against going back to God. And because of this, they brought destruction upon Egypt.

"...Thus says the Lord, Behold, I will give Pharaoh Hophra
king of Egypt into the hand of his enemies and into the hand
of those who seek his life, as I gave Zedekiah king of Judah
into the hand of Nebuchadnezzar king of Babylon, who was
his enemy and sought his life."

Jeremiah 43:30

Our hearts may be fickle, but we can defend against our ever-changing desires by relying on the Holy Spirit and depending on God for answers. When we rely on God over everything and everyone else, we put our hearts in a safe place. We may not always be physically safe, but God will always be with us and use us for His glory.

Jeremiah 45

This chapter jumps back several years earlier, to while Baruch, Jeremiah's scribe is still in Judah. It's during "the fourth year of Jehoiakim the son of Josiah, the king of Judah" (Jeremiah 45:1). Baruch is distraught. We don't get any specifics, but he laments that "the Lord has added sorrow to [his] pain. . . .and [he finds] no rest" (Jeremiah 45:3).

During this time, Egypt and Babylon are battling over Judah. In the thick of the fighting, Baruch ties himself to Jeremiah, of whom people aren't overly fond. In this same year, Baruch helps Jeremiah record all the words that God has given him over the years for Judah so that they may have another chance to repent.

It's no surprise that he's feeling overwhelmed and exhausted. Hard times happen to everyone. We may go through relationships that are particularly draining, or financial difficulties that stretch our faith. God doesn't intend for these moments to break us, but to grow us.

> *"Thus says the Lord, the God of Israel, to you, O Baruch: You said, 'Woe is me! For the Lord has added sorrow to my pain. I am weary with my groaning, and I find no rest.' Thus shall you say to him, Thus says the Lord: Behold, what I have built I am breaking down, and what I have planted I am plucking up—that is, the whole land. And do you seek great things for yourself? Seek them not, for behold, I am bringing disaster upon all flesh, declares the Lord. But I will give you your life as a prize of war in all places to which you may go."*
>
> *Jeremiah 45:2-5*

God knows Baruch's heart. Baruch was seeking approval from the world, something that we all fall prey to. But God reminds him that the only approval he needs to seek is from Him. God promises Baruch hi life. It may not seem like much, but as Christ followers, our lives here are precious. While on this Earth, we can live out God's glory by making disciples. Baruch was worried about the wrong things. God shifted Baruch's focus back to Him, so he could continue to help bring Judah back to their true Father.

Jeremiah 46

There are two separate prophecies in this chapter, as well as a note of encouragement to Judah. The first prophecy was spoken and fulfilled much earlier than the second, in the fourth year of Jehoiakim. The second is a prophecy of the destruction of Egypt, to which Jeremiah is unwillingly taken.

The first prophecy references Egypt being defeated by the Chaldeans. The Egyptian army was an impressive force. But God upsets even the mightiest of nations. He has time and time again defeated the giant by helping the underdog. As we know from previous chapters, the Egyptians retreated and suffered the humiliation of doing so.

I struggle a lot with these war stories. They don't fit neatly into the box into which I try to stuff God. But the truth is, His justice is very much a part of Him. God doesn't exact justice without purpose—that wouldn't be justice at all. He gives people and nations time to repent and only serves justice from a position of righteous discipliner.

Despite my struggle with them, I still find these stories of war very inspiring. I'm especially awed by small bands of armies going against huge armies and prevailing. Most days I feel like a very small army, fighting my own difficulties, sin, or, whatever the struggle of the day may be. When I finally remember that God can defeat the biggest of armies with the smallest of armies, I can rest in His divine strategy and strength. My role is simply to obey His orders.

The Egyptians were warned in the second prophesy that they'd fall subject to Babylon's army yet again. This time, God promises great destruction. Although Egypt deserved justice due to their reliance on their own gods, despite seeing God's mighty hand on and around their nation for years, the ultimate reason for this invasion is because a remnant of Judah fled to Pharaoh instead of to God for protection.

It can be tempting to trust in people over God. People are visible, can physically hold us, and have conversations with us, usually without a need to first silence our mind and heart. Meeting with God is sometimes so abstract that it seems easier to run to a person. God understands, but He wants us to run to Him for security.

> *"Fear not, O Jacob my servant, declares the Lord, for I am with you. I will make a full end of all the nations to which I have driven you, but of you I will not make a full end. I will discipline you in just measure, and I will by no means leave you unpunished."*
>
> *Jeremiah 46:28*

Jeremiah leaves the Israelites with a promise of hope, but also discipline. Generations have slowly faded God out of their lives and when called back, they've rebuked God, saying He wasn't what they needed.

No matter what the world says, we need God desperately. We're called to treasure God in our hearts, to give Him all of us, to obey His word and to strive daily to live more like Him.

Jeremiah 47

For the next several chapters we see God promise to end the nations surrounding Judah. Next are the Philistines, who've long been Israel's enemy.

> *"Thus says the Lord:*
> *Behold, waters are rising out of the north,*
> *and shall become an overflowing torrent;*
> *they shall overflow the land and all that fills it,*
> *the city and those who dwell in it.*
> *Men shall cry out,*
> *and every inhabitant of the land shall wail.*
> *At the noise of the stamping of the hoofs of his stallions,*
> *at the rushing of his chariots, at the rumbling of their wheels,*
> *the fathers look not back to their children,*
> *so feeble are their hands, ..."*

Jeremiah 47:2-3

The Philistines will be so overcome that parents will abandon their children. The invading armies will strike fear into the hearts of the Philistines even before they invade. "So great will be the panic that fathers will abandon children to their fate."[63]

It's hard to imagine being in such a state of panic that you would leave behind those who rely on you for safety, and not even care what they'll face. But the Philistines' trust didn't lie in God, it was in themselves. Their trust was in their own strength and the strength of those around them who may come to their aid. Panic sets in quickly and easily when we see our support crumble. Being able to see and touch what we trust for support is comforting. But these things fade away, whereas God's presence is eternal.

God calls out the sword against the Philistines.

"Ah, sword of the Lord!
How long till you are quiet?
Put yourself into your scabbard;
rest and be still!
How can it be quiet
when the Lord has given it a charge?
Against Ashkelon and against the seashore
he has appointed it."

Jeremiah 47:6-7

We've seen Jeremiah make pleas before for his people to be spared the dire consequences of their sins, and here we see his heart yet again. But he so cares for all people that he "expresses the…earnest desire to see an end of the war, looking with compassion…even upon the Philistines themselves, when their country was made desolate by the sword."[64]

But Jeremiah also knows that God's justice is perfect and when He finally implements it, He does so perfectly. So "while Jeremiah pleads for the divinely-wielded sword to cease its ravages, he is aware that it constitutes God's judgment upon a pagan nation."[65]

Jeremiah 48

Like most of their neighbors, the people of Moab turned to idols instead of God. They believed their idols held more protection than God could, and that they were safe from His response. They've been enjoying safety for years. The prophecy even states that "Moab has been at ease from [its] youth" (Jeremiah 48:11). God had left them alone. His people have been in and around for ages, but Moab has always been on the sidelines.

This didn't stop them from claiming they were better than God. Their pride was one of their biggest downfalls. Pride doesn't get much bigger than when you claim to be better than God. Not only was their pride rampant, it was apparently famous.

We have heard of the pride of Moab—
he is very proud—
of his loftiness, his pride, and his arrogance,
and the haughtiness of his heart.
I know his insolence, declares the Lord;
his boasts are false,
his deeds are false.

Jeremiah 48:29-30

We tend to value pride in our culture. We call ourselves independent when we refuse help, even if we're drowning. We call ourselves confident when we climb over others to get to the top. We consider ourselves better, smarter, stronger, prettier, more talented, and the list goes on, when really, we're just giving into pride.

I struggle with pride the most when it comes to my self-worth. chase vanity instead of accepting myself with confidence in my identity in Christ. And it's drilled into us everywhere in our culture. W are bombarded with images of flawless people with flawless lives. It's all considered worth our time, when really, what does it lead to? Does it help us cling to God?

It's not wrong to put yourself together, to use your gifts, or to improve yourself. We can honor God through these activities, but not when we intend to inflate ourselves. Our self-worth doesn't need to come from anything or anyone but God. And until it comes from God, we will always struggle to find it.

God gave Jeremiah this prophecy against Moab, to tell them of their destruction for their choices. But in the midst of it, Jeremiah does something beautiful: he mourns for them. He's heartbroken over Moab's destruction. He doesn't want it to happen. And from all we see in scripture, neither does God. God desires for the world to turn back to Him.

When we see injustice, we want to see retribution. But God is not only just, He's merciful too. His heart breaks for those who don't turn to Him. Some of the most God honoring times in our lives will be when we forgive and show mercy to those who've done terrible things to us or others.

One of my favorite stories of forgiveness comes from a school shooting in an Amish community. Many children died that day at the hands of a man who wasn't from the community. The families mourned and held a funeral to honor their children, but they also did something completely unexpected. They forgave the man and cared for his widow and family. They reached out to them only hours after the shooting to make sure they were okay, and later to see that their needs were met. They spoke kindly to them and even attended the man's funeral. If that isn't a testament of mercy and forgiveness, I don't know what is.

If Christ-followers were known by our love and mercy instead of our judgement and anger, what impact could it have? That's not to say that we should withhold truth—but it is to say that we should mourn. Let us mourn like Jeremiah, who, while condemning a nation, was also grieved by their sentence.

Jeremiah 49

God declares judgement against nations near Judah who have failed to right themselves with Him. In this chapter, we learn about five of those nations, Ammon, Edom, Syria, Kedar and Hazor, and Elam. Each of these nations has wronged God or his people and are now a part of the widespread judgment of this area.

It's always hard for me to think about God's judgement, so let me start out with some encouragement. It's okay to not fully understand it. I sure don't, not even close. It's a difficult concept, largely because it's God's divine judgment, not human judgement. His judgement is holy. So, hang in there, and ask God for wisdom and clarity.

The first nation addressed is Ammon, a nation near the settlements of Israel, but across the Jordan river. They stole land from parts of Gad—land given by God not by His promise, but at Gad's request. Despite this, He didn't look on Ammon's land grab favorably.

Therefore, behold, the days are coming,
declares the Lord,
when I will cause the battle cry to be heard
against Rabbah of the Ammonites;
it shall become a desolate mound,
and its villages shall be burned with fire;
then Israel shall dispossess those who dispossessed him,
says the Lord.

Jeremiah 49:2

God doesn't just promise judgement on Ammon, He also promises the just return of Israel's lands. But also, at the very end of the prophecy God promises to "restore the fortunes of the Ammonites" (Jeremiah

49:5). What an encouraging thought, that though God breaks them down, He'll also rebuild them.

The second nation is Edom. Edom was "occupied by Esau's descendants"[66] and their kings "were hostile to Israel".[67] It's also clear that they thought of themselves as indestructible.

The horror you inspire has deceived you,
and the pride of your heart,
you who live in the clefts of the rock,
who hold the height of the hill.
Though you make your nest as high as the eagle's,
I will bring you down from there,
declares the Lord.

Jeremiah 49:16

"Edom was evidently well known for two great assets: her wise men and her almost inaccessible strongholds."[68] When our pride swells, we forget our need for God. We believe we're able to deal with life on our own, and that we're indestructible. But no one is beyond God. We all need Him.

The third nation is Syria, and the prophesy is specifically addressed to Damascus, Syria's capital. Damascus has entered a state of fleshly desire in the people's hearts. The city is described as "a city of praise, not to God, but to herself, a city much commended and admired by all strangers that visited it. It was a city of joy, where there was an affluence and confluence of all the delights of the sons of men, and abundance of mirth in the enjoyment of them."[69] The problem is that it's beloved in a way which causes it to be praised above God.

Praise is tainted when it puffs us up and causes us to think we're above God. We then begin to believe that we can do things without Him, that we can control our life and our circumstances, or that we're equal with God. High praise of objects or places can easily turn to idolatry, loving the creation in place of the Creator.

The strangest prophecy concerns Kedar and Hazor. This is a people group who have only what they need. They don't have excessive wealth, and, though they have plenty of livestock to sustain them, they don't own anything for someone to covet. As a result, they don't worry for their safety. So why would they suffer the wrath of God? What good could possibly come from their destruction?

One possible reason is simply that Nebuchadnezzar chose to go after them. Nebuchadnezzar wasn't a man after God's heart. He was a ruler who wanted to conquer others. Even though Nebuchadnezzar was "unrighteous…in doing it, God was righteous in directing it".[70] God can do amazing things with those actions people chose to do merely for harm or their own gain. He can change terrible things into good things. Yes, Hazor and Kedar are described as being unlivable after Nebuchadnezzar's attack, but there is no description of people being killed. They seem to be dispersed instead.

"Rise up, advance against a nation at ease,
that dwells securely,
declares the Lord,
that has no gates or bars,
that dwells alone.
Their camels shall become plunder,
their herds of livestock a spoil.
I will scatter to every wind
those who cut the corners of their hair,
and I will bring their calamity
from every side of them,
declares the Lord.
Hazor shall become a haunt of jackals,
an everlasting waste;
no man shall dwell there;

no man shall sojourn in her."

Jeremiah 49:31-33

The second, and more important reason, the reason they'd be targeted at all, was that they felt safe. They didn't feel they needed God's protection. Their inclusion was, potentially, "for the correcting of an unthankful people, and for warning to a careless world to expect trouble when they seem most safe".[71]

Israel and Judah had decided they didn't need God anymore, and that they didn't need His protection. But we always need His protection. We can't live in continuous comfort and still glorify God. When we put our trust in God, we let our safety be His concern. He protects us—not always how we want, but always how we need.

The final nation is Elam. This nation is similar to Edom in the sense that they celebrate their own might. They treat their king as a god and rely on him instead of the one, true God. The interesting thing about Elam is, at the end of the prophecy, God promises to restore their fortunes, as He did for Ammon. This turns out to be a much longer and more fascinating story.

> *When Cyrus had destroyed Babylon, brought the empire into the hands of the Persians, the Elamites no doubt returned in triumph out of all the countries whither they were scattered, and settled again in their own country. But this promise [to restore their fortune] was to have its full and principal accomplishment in the days of the Messiah, when we find the Elamites particularly among those who, when the Holy Ghost was given, heard spoken in their own tongues the wonderful works of God (Acts 2:9-11), and that is the most desirable return of the captivity.[72]*

That story gives me goosebumps. After thousands of years, God restored their fortunes and brought Elamites to Him through Jesus' disciples. God doesn't think in the short term like us. He thinks in the extremely long term! Even though we may not be able to see what good can come from difficult things in our life, if we have faith that God is in control and is good, we can trust that there are amazing things to come.

Aren't you glad you stuck through that chapter? What an ending, an ending that's a beginning?!

Jeremiah 50

Here begins a two-chapter prophesy against Babylon, saved last for destruction. However, this prophecy isn't just about Babylon. This prophecy moves back and forth between the destruction of Babylon and the redemption of Israel. It may seem odd that God would intertwine the two, but part of Israel's redemption is Babylon's destruction.

> *"Though you rejoice, though you exult,*
> *O plunderers of my heritage,*
> *though you frolic like a heifer in the pasture,*
> *and neigh like stallions,*
> *your mother shall be utterly shamed,*
> *and she who bore you shall be disgraced.*
> *Behold, she shall be the last of the nations,*
> *a wilderness, a dry land, and a desert.*
>
> *Jeremiah 50:11-12*

Babylon rejoiced at the destruction of Judah. This is one of the main reasons why they will be destroyed. God may have used them to correct Judah, but this was not something God took pleasure in. I imagine it pained Him to see anyone excited about His beloved nation's torment.

God doesn't take pleasure in breaking us down. But He does take great pleasure in rebuilding us. He enjoys shaping our character to be closer to His holiness so we can be brighter lights in this ever-deepening darkness. God wants us to be like Him.

Another major reason for Babylon's destruction is they've attacked everyone else. God calls them "the hammer of the whole earth" (Jeremiah 50:23). They annihilated nation after nation and have grown fat off the plunder. They've turned to their gods instead of God throughout their existence. And now, with this great and comfortable wealth, there is little chance they'd turn to God.

When we're wealthy, the times we bring ourselves to depend on God become intermittent to non-existent, essentially relegating Him to a little corner on Sunday mornings. Though it's lovely to not have to worry where your next meal will come from or whether there will be a roof over your head for the night, it's when you rely on God for the big things that you learn how faithful He is.

Israel gets one particularly special blessing in this prophesy—they get a full pardon.

In those days and in that time, declares the Lord, iniquity shall be sought in Israel, and there shall be none, and sin in Judah, and none shall be found, for I will pardon those whom I leave as a remnant.

Jeremiah 50:20

None shall be found. No scars, no marks in the dust, no trace of what they perpetrated against God. He'll completely forget. When I think of the slate that God not only wiped clean, but also made new for me, I am moved with a deep reverence and gratitude. The fact that He'd love me enough to let me become a new creation, not just a patched one, shows His intimate care of me. He desires for me to be full, through the powerful sacrifice of His Son.

Jeremiah 51

Babylon has been "a golden cup" (Jeremiah 51:7) and a "hammer and weapon of war" (Jeremiah 51:20) while in God's hands. The nation brought both prosperity and destruction, depending on how God was using them. But throughout that time, God planned to eventually destroy Babylon; at the very end of this chapter we learn that this prophesy was spoken and recorded in the fourth year of Zedekiah's reign—seven years before Jerusalem fell to Babylon.

There are a lot of questions that race through my mind in this part of Jeremiah. Why would God use a nation? Isn't that cruel? How can so much destruction be permissible, let alone good?

The reasoning isn't always visible in the moment-by-moment narrative. It's in the big picture. God's actions often seem incomplete in the moment but later reveal a depth of plan that can only be divine. God isn't confined by human conceptions and His use of people or nations in terrible acts may be a necessary step for their eventual repentance.

Consider Jesus' ancestry. David killed Bathsheba's husband to hide his adultery. And yet, it was in David and Bathsheba's line that Jesus was born. God redeems even the unredeemable.

God uses people and nations in interesting ways. Throughout this book we've seen Babylon as a major player and have seen how God has directed them depending on the actions of other nations. When Judah refuses to listen to Him, even after years of patient grace, He allows Babylon to destroy them. Babylon plunders and levels much of the nation. Yet, while Judah has all but entirely forsaken God, He's still with them and promises eventual redemption.

Babylon lives in relative peace, having conquered most of their neighbors. Jeremiah prophesies that the king will feel so secure he won't even realize he's being attacked.

The warriors of Babylon have ceased fighting;
they remain in their strongholds;
their strength has failed;
they have become women;
her dwellings are on fire;
her bars are broken.
One runner runs to meet another,
and one messenger to meet another,
to tell the king of Babylon
that his city is taken on every side;
the fords have been seized,
the marshes are burned with fire,
and the soldiers are in panic.

Jeremiah 51:30-32

The final words of this prophecy are "thus far are the words of Jeremiah" (Jeremiah 51:64). This chapter ends the prophesies of Jeremiah. Though this prophesy took place much earlier, it's placed last as the destruction of Babylon was saved for the end. Similar to the mass exodus from Egypt, this exodus will start a new chapter for Judah.

Jeremiah 52

After all the brain-racking prophesies, this final chapter is almost anti-climactic. But that's because it's not the finale—it's a beginning. This chapter rehashes the details of Jerusalem's destruction as a type of introduction to Lamentations,[73] which some believe Jeremiah also wrote.

It's hard to say whether or not this last chapter is part of Jeremiah's writings, or someone else's. It seems likely it's from the same writer of 2 Kings.[74] The main point of this chapter is to redirect your focus. It can be hard to see the Bible as a whole when we focus on specific books, but it's important to do so that we can get to the meat of them. It's also extremely important to remember that all the books fit together as, if I may borrow a Sunday school term, God's Big Story.

This is a good reminder that our lives aren't just ours. Though we may have to focus on our own lives at times to make sure we're living within God's calling, we must always remember that we're part of His big story, too. Our lives fit in with others to make up God's story. Our journeys, our consequences, and our triumphs are not ours alone. We aren't meant to walk, struggle or rejoice alone. We're meant to do all things within community.

This chapter is strictly a historical account of what happened to Jerusalem, though it doesn't pick up until its complete destruction. The book of Jeremiah is prophecy specifically for that time in Jerusalem. Since God's word is alive and not static, we can always find things in scripture that relate to us now. But we also need to be careful to not apply that which doesn't apply. In other words, we can't read the book of Jeremiah as a prophesy for this century and try to connect every little thing to our lives today.

As I read through many of the prophesies, there were things that sounded like they could have been written for today. Part of that observation is because history repeats itself, and we're still full of sinful nature.

We also still have a difficult time obeying God. If I tried to live my life as though I was living during Jeremiah's prophesies, I'd miss a lot of what God wants to do with me today. If I understand why God sent the prophesies in the first place, and learn from the Judeans' responses to them, my life will reflect God's glory more fully.

So, go. Respond to God as His Spirit speaks to you and live life for His glory.

Notes

Jeremiah 1

1. Fortify. (n.d.) In Merriam-Webster's collegiate dictionary. Retrieved from http://www.merriam-webster.com/dictionary/fortify

2. Harrison, R.K. Jeremiah & Lamentations. InterVarsity Press,1973. See page 50.

Jeremiah 2

3. Henry, Matthew. Commentaries on Jeremiah. Scriptura Press, 2015. See page xxviii.

4. Kidner, Derek. The Message of Jeremiah. InterVarsity Press, 1987. See page 33.

Jeremiah 4

5. Harrison, R.K. Jeremiah & Lamentations. InterVarsity Press,1973. See page 68.

Jeremiah 6

6. Harrison, R.K. Jeremiah & Lamentations. InterVarsity Press,1973. See page 83.

Jeremiah 7

7. Harrison, R.K. Jeremiah & Lamentations. InterVarsity Press,1973. See page 86.

Jeremiah 8

8. Kidner, Derek. The Message of Jeremiah. InterVarsity Press, 1987. See page 52.

Jeremiah 9

9. Henry, Matthew. Commentaries on Jeremiah. Scriptura Press, 2015. See page ccii.

10. Henry, Matthew. Commentaries on Jeremiah. Scriptura Press, 2015. See page ccxi.

11. Kidner, Derek. The Message of Jeremiah. InterVarsity Press, 1987. See page 56.

Jeremiah 13

12. Henry, Matthew. Commentaries on Jeremiah. Scriptura Press, 2015. See page cxlii.

13. Harrison, R.K. Jeremiah & Lamentations. InterVarsity Press,1973. See page 99.

Jeremiah 16

14. Harrison, R.K. Jeremiah & Lamentations. InterVarsity Press,1973. See page 104.

Jeremiah 17

15. Henry, Matthew. Commentaries on Jeremiah. Scriptura Press, 2015. See page clxxxi.

Jeremiah 18

16. Henry, Matthew. Commentaries on Jeremiah. Scriptura Press, 2015. See page cxciii.
17. Kidner, Derek. The Message of Jeremiah. InterVarsity Press, 1987. See page 76.

Jeremiah 19

18. Henry, Matthew. Commentaries on Jeremiah. Scriptura Press, 2015. See page cciv.
19. Harrison, R.K. Jeremiah & Lamentations. InterVarsity Press,1973. See page 111.
20. Harrison, R.K. Jeremiah & Lamentations. InterVarsity Press,1973. See page 110.
21. Henry, Matthew. Commentaries on Jeremiah. Scriptura Press, 2015. See pages ccv-ccvi.

Jeremiah 20

22. Harrison, R.K. Jeremiah & Lamentations. InterVarsity Press,1973. See page 113.
23. Henry, Matthew. Commentaries on Jeremiah. Scriptura Press, 2015. See page ccix.

Jeremiah 21

24. Harrison, R.K. Jeremiah & Lamentations. InterVarsity Press,1973. See page 112.
25. Henry, Matthew. Commentaries on Jeremiah. Scriptura Press, 2015. See page ccxix.
26. Henry, Matthew. Commentaries on Jeremiah. Scriptura Press, 2015. See page ccxix.

Jeremiah 22

27. Henry, Matthew. Commentaries on Jeremiah. Scriptura Press, 2015. See page ccxviii.
28. Henry, Matthew. Commentaries on Jeremiah. Scriptura Press, 2015. See page ccxxviii.

Jeremiah 24

29. Harrison, R.K. Jeremiah & Lamentations. InterVarsity Press,1973. See page 124.

Jeremiah 27

30. Henry, Matthew. Commentaries on Jeremiah. Scriptura Press, 2015. See page cclxx.

Jeremiah 28

31. Kidner, Derek. The Message of Jeremiah. InterVarsity Press, 1987. See page 99.
32. Henry, Matthew. Commentaries on Jeremiah. Scriptura Press, 2015. See page cclxxvii.

Jeremiah 29

33. Henry, Matthew. Commentaries on Jeremiah. Scriptura Press, 2015. See page cclxxxviii.

Jeremiah 30

34. Henry, Matthew. Commentaries on Jeremiah. Scriptura Press, 2015. See page cclxxxix.
35. Henry, Matthew. Commentaries on Jeremiah. Scriptura Press, 2015. See page ccxc.

Jeremiah 31

36. Henry, Matthew. Commentaries on Jeremiah. Scriptura Press, 2015. See page cccix.
37. Henry, Matthew. Commentaries on Jeremiah. Scriptura Press, 2015. See page cccix.

Jeremiah 32

38. Kidner, Derek. The Message of Jeremiah. InterVarsity Press, 1987. See page 112.
39. Henry, Matthew. Commentaries on Jeremiah. Scriptura Press, 2015. See page cccxviii.

Jeremiah 33

40. Henry, Matthew. Commentaries on Jeremiah. Scriptura Press, 2015. See page cccxxiv.

Jeremiah 34

41. Kidner, Derek. The Message of Jeremiah. InterVarsity Press, 1987. See page 117.

Jeremiah 35

42. Kidner, Derek. The Message of Jeremiah. InterVarsity Press, 1987. See page 118.
43. Henry, Matthew. Commentaries on Jeremiah. Scriptura Press, 2015. See page cccxlii.

Jeremiah 36

44. Henry, Matthew. Commentaries on Jeremiah. Scriptura Press, 2015. See page cccxlvi.

Jeremiah 37

45. Henry, Matthew. Commentaries on Jeremiah. Scriptura Press, 2015. See page cccliv.
46. Henry, Matthew. Commentaries on Jeremiah. Scriptura Press, 2015. See page ccclvi.
47. Henry, Matthew. Commentaries on Jeremiah. Scriptura Press, 2015. See page ccclvi.

Jeremiah 38

48. Henry, Matthew. Commentaries on Jeremiah. Scriptura Press, 2015. See page ccclix.
49. Henry, Matthew. Commentaries on Jeremiah. Scriptura Press, 2015. See page ccclix.
50. Kidner, Derek. The Message of Jeremiah. InterVarsity Press, 1987. See page 125.

Jeremiah 39

51. Henry, Matthew. Commentaries on Jeremiah. Scriptura Press, 2015. See page ccclxvii.
52. Henry, Matthew. Commentaries on Jeremiah. Scriptura Press, 2015. See page ccclxvii.
53. Henry, Matthew. Commentaries on Jeremiah. Scriptura Press, 2015. See page ccclxviii.

Jeremiah 40

54. Henry, Matthew. Commentaries on Jeremiah. Scriptura Press, 2015. See page ccclxxi.
55. Henry, Matthew. Commentaries on Jeremiah. Scriptura Press, 2015. See page ccclxxiii-ccclxxiv.
56. Henry, Matthew. Commentaries on Jeremiah. Scriptura Press, 2015. See page ccclxxiv.

Jeremiah 42

57. Henry, Matthew. Commentaries on Jeremiah. Scriptura Press, 2015. See page ccclxxx.
58. Harrison, R.K. Jeremiah & Lamentations. InterVarsity Press,1973. See page 163.

Jeremiah 43

59. Kidner, Derek. The Message of Jeremiah. InterVarsity Press, 1987. See page 131.
60. Henry, Matthew. Commentaries on Jeremiah. Scriptura Press, 2015. See page ccclxxxvii.
61. Kidner, Derek. The Message of Jeremiah. InterVarsity Press, 1987. See page 131.
62. Henry, Matthew. Commentaries on Jeremiah. Scriptura Press, 2015. See page ccclxxxviii.

Jeremiah 47

63. Harrison, R.K. Jeremiah & Lamentations. InterVarsity Press,1973. See page 173.
64. Henry, Matthew. Commentaries on Jeremiah. Scriptura Press, 2015. See page cdviii.
65. Harrison, R.K. Jeremiah & Lamentations. InterVarsity Press,1973. See page 173.

Jeremiah 49

66. Harrison, R.K. Jeremiah & Lamentations. InterVarsity Press,1973. See page 179.
67. Harrison, R.K. Jeremiah & Lamentations. InterVarsity Press,1973. See page 180.
68. Kidner, Derek. The Message of Jeremiah. InterVarsity Press, 1987. See page 144.
69. Henry, Matthew. Commentaries on Jeremiah. Scriptura Press, 2015. See page cdxxiii.
70. Henry, Matthew. Commentaries on Jeremiah. Scriptura Press, 2015. See page cdxxiv.
71. Henry, Matthew. Commentaries on Jeremiah. Scriptura Press, 2015. See page cdxxiv.
72. Henry, Matthew. Commentaries on Jeremiah. Scriptura Press, 2015. See page cdxxvi.

73. Henry, Matthew. Commentaries on Jeremiah. Scriptura Press, 2015. See page cdxlix.

74. Harrison, R.K. Jeremiah & Lamentations. InterVarsity Press,1973. See page 190.

References

The Bible. English Standard Version. Crossway Bibles, 2007.

Guzik, David. "Study Guide for Jeremiah 36." Blue Letter Bible. 21 Feb, 2017. Web. 15 Oct, 2018. <https://www.blueletterbible.org/Comm/guzik_david/StudyGuide2017-Jer/Jer-36.cfm>.

Harrison, R.K. Jeremiah & Lamentations. InterVarsity Press, 1973.

Henry, Matthew. Commentaries on Jeremiah. Scriptura Press, 2015.

Kidner, Derek. The Message of Jeremiah. InterVarsity Press, 1987.

Special Thanks

To Stephen Marrano for his insight and suggestions regarding the theological material and word choices for this book;

To Courtney McLean for editing the first draft and helping to shape the content;

To Mike Gorter for his amazing design of the cover and formatting of this book;

And to Aaron Heise for editing the final draft, shaping and refining each chapter, and formatting and putting together this book so it could be published. Thank you for also being my biggest supporter and encourgament through this process.

Made in the USA
Coppell, TX
09 November 2020

41036613R00080